APO PADI

(An Autobiography)

by

CLIFFORD E. BARRY NOBES, S.T.D.

New Day Publishers
Quezon City
1988

BV
3382
. N63
A3
1988 .
C. 1

DEDICATION

For Florence Moore Nobes, who for more than fifty years has put up with me, sharing adventures in all parts of the world, partner with me in many works for God, and without whom life would indeed have been bleak. I thank God daily that she shared life with me, giving much and receiving little—but that is Florence.

PROLOGUE

It had been an ordinary day, like most days which had passed since the Japanese invasion of the Philippines had virtually isolated our Mountain Province. We had heard no news, and when news is lacking, rumors abound. Those which reached us at All Saints Mission in Bontoc we shared eagerly. We had, of course, noted that as the weeks dragged on these reports became more and more absurd. A huge fleet of American warships, convoying dozens of troop transports, was speeding across the Pacific. Thousands of Chinese infantrymen had landed on the beaches of northern Luzon and were advancing down the Cagayan River Valley. An army composed of Australian and New Zealand units had landed in Mindanao and was pushing northward. American bombers, launched from carriers, had raided Manila and other Japanese strongholds on Luzon. And so on.

But we became more and more disheartened when it became apparent that these reports and others too ludicrous to repeat were based on nothing but hope. The only truth was that the Japanese invaders were solidly in possession of all parts of the Philippine Archipelago, so we had agreed to believe nothing until we could hear it from a uniformed representative of the United States Army.

This day, as the afternoon shadows lengthened and darkness fell, my wife and I were at home, Florence in the kitchen preparing the evening meal, and I preparing for Sunday's service when I was startled to hear a quiet rap on the front door. It was the mayor of the town. He was accompanied by a bedraggled American soldier, wearing rags which had once been a uniform. I ushered the two men into the house quickly. The mayor, obviously nervous, refused my invitation to remain, telling me that he had delivered my countryman into my hands and that he considered his job done. First peering out of a crack in the blackout curtains to make sure that there was no one on the road on which the rectory faced, he slipped out of the door and was gone.

The soldier, now alone with Florence and me, told us that he was a captain in the Army Air Corps. He had been on reconnaissance in an obsolete pursuit plane over Northern Luzon, near the mouth of the Cagayan River, when a Japanese Zero had emerged from a cloud bank, and after a short and one-sided dog-fight, had shot him down.

He had bailed out of his crippled aircraft and had managed to control the direction of his descent before his parachute was ripped to

3

shreds by the machine gun fire of his victorious adversary. Then he plummeted into the middle of the river.

The Japanese airman made several low passes over the area, strafing the river surface each time. Finally, after apparently exhausting his ammunition—a period of time which seemed an eternity to his quarry —he flew away. The American had survived by remaining submerged in the muddy water between passes, daring to surface only when the fading engine sounds indicated that he was temporarily safe. Then he would gasp for air and dive as deeply as he could at the next approach. His dives were dangerously shallow by the time the final pass was made and he was near the end of his endurance when his head broke water for the last time.

After visually measuring the distances to the river banks, and in spite of his exhaustion, for no reason that he could remember he elected to swim to the farther shore. While he lay on the beach, recovering his breath and congratulating himself on the amazing fact that he was still alive, he was astounded and delighted to see an American soldier approaching. The newcomer had been an interested observer of the dogfight, the plunge into the river, and the fiery crash of the American plane into a field on the other side of the river. After introducing himself, and expressing his surprise and relief that his countryman seemed more or less in one piece, he told the downed pilot that while their bank of the Cagayan was still in American hands, the opposite one had been seized by the Japanese a few days before.

"It was then," continued the captain, "that I became convinced of the efficacy of prayer, because believe me, Padre, from the time that Jap came out of the clouds until I pulled myself up on the river bank, I had prayed constantly. And I learned something else that morning. I learned that war is dangerous to one's personal well-being. That son-of-a-bitch tried as hard as he could to kill me. From now on this war is no longer just between the Japanese Empire and the good old U.S.A. Now it's personal—between Japan and me."

Soon the pair on the river bank were joined by other Americans who told the waterlogged pilot that they knew of no nearby units of the American Army other than their own, a small contingent of Signal Corpsmen. Their orders were to set up a listening post in the area to monitor southbound traffic from Japan. Because of the strength of the invaders, they had not been able to do this so they were now just lying low waiting to withdraw to the South as soon as authority to abandon their mission could be obtained.

All they could do for the flyer was feed him, give him a map of the northern end of Luzon, and let him rest until he felt able to undertake the difficult hike through the jungle in the general direction of Bontoc. There, they told him, he would find an Episcopal Church mission and possibly some sort of transportation southward to an American unit. They advised him to stay off the roads, which were

4

patrolled by the Japanese, and, so far as possible, to travel only by night. They then gave him a few emergency rations and a compass and sent him on his way.

He had been a week in the woods, and he was now completely exhausted. After finishing his tale, he luxuriated in a hot bath, consumed a prodigious hot meal, and collapsed into bed where he remained for 24 hours.

It didn't take much the next day to convince him that he had better let me take him to the Provincial Hospital in Bontoc to receive treatment for his many abrasions, some of which were obviously infected.

About a week later the Japanese arrived in Bontoc in force. There had been a foraging party which had come into town a month before, but they had simply stripped the two stores in the town of everything edible, butchered a few animals, stolen some of our food, and then withdrawn to Cervantes whence they had come. This second group had come to stay, and I was concerned for the American flyer whom I had left at the hospital. It was several years later that I learned that the Filipino staff had managed to sneak him out of the hospital and arranged for him to be cared for by various Filipino families. Eventually he was able to rejoin the remnant of his unit and to resume his war against the Japanese Empire. When I located him at Wright Air Field in Ohio after my return to the States, he told me that he had been shot down twice more after which he was sent home where he took up the task of training other fliers to avoid similar experiences.

It was adventures such as this which made my time in the Philippines from 1931 through 1945 so exciting. Now, half a century later, I find that my memories are rapidly fading. I cannot even remember the name of the pilot of whom I have spoken. And there were many equally exciting experiences in the years I served as a missionary in the Islands before the Japanese invasion. So, I want to write of that time which is past. Some of the people in my story are still living, but many have died. Even the places where all of this took place have been so altered by the passing years that in some cases all that persist are the place names. However, despite all this change, there is one enduring constant, and that is the Igorot people.

At the beginning of my narrative, these people with few exceptions were living simple lives in a primitive society which had not changed in untold centuries. They lived in ignorance of the causes of most natural phenomena, like storms, lightning and thunder, drought and earthquakes. Equally mysterious to them were the reasons for personal misfortunes, such as illnesses, blindness, and other afflictions of the body.

Fear of nature was one consequence of this ignorance. Superstition was another. Misfortunes resulting from natural disasters, as well as from personal afflictions, were ascribed to the machinations of supernatural spirits. To alleviate the trouble caused by their visitations, they had only prayer and propitiatory sacrifices. Their fear was oppressive and actually ruled their lives. When they sought, all they could find in their own culture was the mumbo-jumbo of old men and women of the village, and the assurance from them that when the spirits responsible were properly identified and placated, the troubles would cease.

Not satisfied with this, they began to seek better answers to their problems. They turned to people other than their own tribesmen. They invited people alien to their culture to help them.

The old ways which had isolated and stifled them for so many centuries began to erode. They realized that customs were inadequate for the new world which they now glimpsed, and into which they wished to move.

So, eagerly and willingly by the younger and more adventurous among them, reluctantly and fearfully by their elders, they abandoned the old and started adapting to the new.

Then the greatest war ever waged on this planet made a battlefield of what had been their remote and beautiful homeland. A primitive race which was scarcely emerging from an archaic culture was set down in a century which itself was in a state of flux. People still not accustomed to the sight and sound of automobiles now saw squadrons of airplanes crisscrossing the skies, and dropping death on people below.

The aliens in their midst had responded to their invitation to help them extricate themselves from the chains of their ancient culture. Now their tutors dreaded the conflagration which was about to erupt because they knew it would exacerbate the confrontation between the old and the new and they could not be sure that the Igorot could cope. Yet they knew that if the Igorot were not properly prepared for the new life, he would be trampled in the stampede to the civilization into which he had to move.

But time showed that they had done their work well. The Igorot moved deftly from his primitive ineptitude into patterns demanded by the new times—demands intensified by war.

This recital is the story of my life when I lived among them during these critical years. But it will also show, I hope, how far the Igorot had to come to take his place in the world of today.

I am sure that it is partly due to the fact that we alien tutors had encouraged them to be proud of their heritage that the Igorot race did not lose its identity and merely merge with the more advanced tribal groups which surrounded them. Freed from their imprisonment in an archaic and totally inadequate culture, Igorots are now making their contribution to the larger society which they have joined.

My depiction of this momentous time must grow out of my own experiences and observations. Others could probably tell the story of the transition better than I, but they cannot tell *my* story. To be sure, there were other agencies operating during this change-over. But, I submit that the missionaries played the dominant role because they had respect for the Igorot as he had been while helping him shape himself into the person he could be.

Even now, half a century later, as I reflect upon all of this, I am amazed at the rapidity of the transformation, and I am grateful that I was privileged to play a small part in the events of those historic days. So, before my memory fails completely, I feel compelled to write of those years.

One day one of my grandchildren may say to me, "Grandpa, what did you do in the Philippines? Were you there when the Japanese came?" I do not want to reply that I have forgotten those exciting times. I would rather say, "Here is a story called *Apo Padi*, and it tells you all about that time, and about me, because your grandfather is 'Apo Padi.'"

CHAPTER I

The excitement attendant upon the sailing of an ocean liner is unique, and has changed little over the years. The ship may have been moored at the dock for days, but the confusion at the pier on sailing day is such that it seems that everyone who wants to put anything aboard has waited until the last minute.

Passenger luggage not intended for use during the voyage accumulates in untidy mounds on the pier. Pieces which will be needed during the trip are thrown into another heap. Huge winches on the dock snarl and hiss as their drums wind and unwind the cables. Gradually the piles of freight and luggage diminish in size as the laden nets drop their cargo into the holds.

In the meanwhile, cabin stewards scurry about picking over the hand luggage. They hasten up the gangplank burdened with four, five or six pieces which they drop on the nearest open deck space for later distribution to the proper cabins. The important thing at this point is to transfer everything from the wharf to the ship so that the vessel can start its voyage.

Passengers crowding the shoreside rails call out last-minute messages to those who came to see them off. Excitement mounts as the harbor pilot comes aboard and is escorted to the bridge. A steward goes through the ship's companionways banging a gong and crying out, "All ashore who are going ashore!" and there is a rush to the gangway.

The longshoremen who have been operating the cranes yield their places to the ship's crew. Other sailors begin closing the hatches and start shipping the booms. The men on the pier lift the hawsers off the bollards and cast them into the greasy water of the harbor, and the sailors haul them aboard ship, coiling them as they do, so that they will run out without fouling the next time the ship must be moored.

In the meanwhile the tugs which will nose the ship into the channel have been positioning themselves fore and aft. Finally, with all the dignity of an archbishop at the end of an ecclesiastical procession, the company's agent, who had been closeted with the freight master and the captain, emerges from the interior of the ship and struts down the gangway, which is then hauled aboard. The passengers scream out their final farewells to their friends on the pier. Handkerchiefs flutter, the ship's deep-throated voice warns others in the harbor that it is about to commence its voyage, and at last the vessel, under its own power, moves down the channel.

On a rainy afternoon in November 1931, I was on board the Dollar liner *President Madison* as she started her voyage from Seattle to the Orient. I was as excited as anyone else aboard, even though I had made more than a dozen crossings of the Atlantic as an ordinary seaman while working my way through college, and I well knew the routine of an ocean liner's departure. My excitement was due rather to the fact that I was aboard as a passenger, not as a crew member, and I was embarking upon a voyage which would take me away from home for at least six years.

Trans-Pacific air routes for passengers had not yet been established, so I had booked passage aboard a ship which would call at ports in Japan and China before reaching Manila. No other ocean voyage I had made had lasted more than a week. This one would take three weeks.

From the time I had entered Columbia College in New York City in the fall of 1923, I had been looking forward to ordination in the Episcopal Church. I had always assumed that I would become a parish priest, exercising my ministry as a pastor in some American setting. But at General Theological Seminary in Chelsea Square in New York City, other ways of serving in the ministry had become known to me. Each spring members of the senior class would talk excitedly about offers of employment that had come their way.

Some were offered curacies in large parishes. Others expected to start as vicars of small congregations. A few looked forward to working as chaplains in hospitals, prisons, educational institutions, or in the military. A few opted for service in the foreign missionary fields of the Church, and still fewer felt the call to serve God and man as monks in one of the several religious orders within the Episcopal Church. The range of possibilities seemed endless.

Of course, one's bishop had first call on his candidates' services. No one could be ordained deacon, the first step toward the goal of priesthood, without a "title," that is, without a position to which he could go. Some bishops, usually those in large dioceses, managed to get around this requirement by designating their unemployed young men as "chaplains to the ordinary." Thus, the man had a "title" and this permitted him to be ordained and then to await suitable employment. So it was with me.

It had been my thought that along with two other newly ordained men we might establish an "associate mission" in the Missionary District of Salina, which was composed of the sparsely populated counties of Western Kansas. Few towns out there were large enough to maintain a self-supporting Episcopal parish. However, we three thought that if we could share household expenses by living in the same house, we would further benefit by being able to share experiences. We could thus save money for the district while simultaneously becoming more effective than if we attempted to live in three different locations.

9

I told my parents who lived in an apartment close to the Seminary of my hopes. They were startled. "Kansas? Isn't that where Dodge City is? The place where cattle rustlers and lawmen shoot it out every once in a while?" (My parents had never been west of New Jersey and imagined that the Cavalry still protected Kansas frontier towns from marauding Indians.)

The Bishop of Salina came to our home for tea one day to assure my mother that his district was indeed a civilized region of the United States. She listened politely but when he left she said to me, "Of course he has to say things like that if he is going to lure any daft young men out into that wilderness."

My parents' dismay was even greater a little later when I told them that I had refused a curacy in a large Boston parish. Towards the end of my senior year at Seminary Dean Fosbroke had summoned me to his office and told me that he had nominated me for a Fellowship which would permit me to continue my studies at the Seminary while serving as a tutor for first- and second-year students. He said that he and the faculty members hoped that I would accept, and that I would use part of my time preparing an outline of an introductory course in Ethics and Moral Theology. The Dean also said that while he could not make a firm promise, he thought that there was a good possibility that he could get another fellowship for me after a year or two at Chelsea Square, which would permit me to do further work in the field of ethics in either Scotland or Germany. Although I was not convinced that the academic life was for me, I accepted this offer in the knowledge that it would give me time to try to ascertain my real preferences for my life's work.

And yet it was not at Chelsea Square, nor in Kansas nor Boston that I started my work as an ordained clergyman. Shortly before my graduation, there came to the Seminary a priest who was on furlough from his post in the Mountain Province of the Philippine Islands. He was looking for someone who would train young men of his area for ordination. The Dean had suggested he talk to me.

Father Rose was a master of the soft sell. He "just happened" to have with him an album of photographs of the Mountain Province in Northern Luzon, through which he invited me to leaf as he talked about his hope of establishing a seminary. His tales of life in this remote and exotic part of the world intrigued me, as did his enthusiasm over the opportunity for doing something important and worthwhile. In effect, he was asking me to take a job which would result in the abolition of this job and the creation of a Church staffed by its own nationals, as had happened in China and Japan.

I told him that I was interested but that I would have to take time to consider all the possibilities which had opened to me and to look further into the history of and present conditions in the Philippine Islands. As he rose to leave I noticed a faint but knowing smile which seemed to say, "I have him hooked."

With a warm handshake he told me that he would be in the New York area for another week and that he would return for my answer before leaving. Although I believe now that my decision had already been made subconsciously, I spent a good deal of time during that week in the chapel seeking divine guidance. I also spent a lot of time at the New York Public Library reading all I could find on the Mountain Province of the Philippines. I made good use, too, of the resources at the Church Mission House where I was permitted to read reports from missionaries in the field.

The Episcopal Church's work in the Sagada area had started in the early 1900's, and had grown so rapidly that it was now perhaps the most successful, from every point of view, of any of the Church's overseas missions.

There are basically two ways of developing a large group of converts in a heathen area. One favored by the great Jesuit missionary, Francis Xavier, is to baptize people after very brief instruction in the Faith, aiming at the creation of a favorable environment for the growth of a Christian enclave in pagan surroundings and then to work hard with the children of the nominal Christians. Another method is to establish a catechumenate and over a long period of time train the candidates for baptism in every aspect of the Faith, and finally, when they have indicated their desire to become Christian and have promised to abandon all heathen ways, to baptize them. This method obviously takes much longer than that used by St. Francis Xavier, but it makes for a solidly based Christian community.

The most obvious advantage of the Xavierian approach is that a climate favorable to Christian expansion is quickly established. The disadvantage is that the converts in the first generation do not really know what the demands of their new religion are, and there is danger of having a syncretic religion—one which is a fusion of two different bodies of belief. The real hopes of the missionaries, then, must lie with the second or third generation of Christians.

Reading of the rapid and enormous growth of the Mission of St. Mary the Virgin in the northern mountains of the Philippines, I suspected that the Xavierian method had been employed. The Mission had grown so quickly under the leadership of John Staunton that it could not have been otherwise. He was well aware of the fact that the days of isolation for the Igorots were drawing to a close. The twentieth century was upon them and he felt that the sooner the Igorots regarded Christianity as "their" religion, the sooner would they be ready to meet the challenges and the dangers of this new century. For these reasons, and in spite of the risk of creating a diluted brand of Christianity, he had adopted Francis Xavier's approach.

In those early years of the twentieth century the results were as he had hoped. Converts were numbered by the thousands.

11

Father Staunton was educated as a civil engineer before he became a priest. He envisioned Sagada as a training center for schooling Igorots in trades of the civilization which was engulfing them.

Sagada became the mother station for a far-flung group of satellite outstations. Schooling ran from the primary grades through four years of high school. The young people were taught useful skills. Under the tutelage of Japanese stoneworkers whom Father Staunton had brought to Sagada, quarrying was conducted on a large scale. The limestone blocks thus obtained were used in the extensive building operations Father Staunton had undertaken. A stone church was built. A print shop was set up, as was a photography studio. Father Staunton filled the mail boxes of a growing list of interested Episcopalians in the States with pamphlets describing the opportunities which awaited the Church in this new field, and soliciting their contributions to finance the ambitious operations which were underway. A saw mill was constructed. Young Igorots learned the mysteries of plumbing.

In the meanwhile, the girls were not forgotten. They had learned to weave by watching their mothers, but now they became skilled in making lace, too. The products of their labors were sold through helpful parishes in the States.

To supervise the secular and religious training of the women and girls of the area, Father Staunton had recruited the Sisters of the Community of St. Mary, an Episcopal religious order for women, the mother house for which was at Peekskill, New York. It was hoped that the order would be able to keep the Convent at Sagada supplied with at least four sisters.

But in 1929 a tragic accident upset this plan. One of the native girls employed in the kitchen of the Convent put sodium fluoride instead of baking powder into some food she was preparing. When the three nuns then in residence became violently ill, medical help was summoned from the government hospital in Bontoc. Two of the sisters died. Sketchy reports of the incident which reached Peekskill caused the Mother Superior to think that the poisoning was deliberate, and she recalled the surviving sister. So the Convent stood empty and the work which had been handled by the sisters was shared by lay women on the station staff. It was several years before a full complement of four sisters returned to resume the order's work in Sagada.

Until then the normal staff of appointed missionaries at Sagada consisted of three priests, three teachers, two or three nurses, one general manager of the business affairs of the station and the wives and children of these workers.

In addition there were about a dozen Igorot teachers, nurses and dispensary workers, several craftsmen, such as carpenters, plumbers, stone masons, and a farrier to take care of the seven or eight horses the mission kept to provide transportation for the priests to reach the outstations. There was also a storekeeper with the responsibility of purchasing and storing supplies for the staff and the boarding school children. So even without the nuns, it was a sizeable group which lived in this central station at Sagada.

To support all of this work it was necessary to solicit "special gifts" over and above the amount allowed in the budget of the National Church. The many accomplishments of the Mission were well publicized in the mailings which went out of Sagada, and the result was a steady stream of dollars flowing into the station.

In fact, missionaries in other areas complained to the National Council that their work was hampered by the fact that when they appealed for gifts, those to whom they directed their requests would often reply that they had given their missionary support to Sagada and could do no more. Restrictions on solicitations were then ordered by the National Council. Before these became effective, however, Episcopalians had become aware of the efforts in and around Sagada, and support continued to come in the form of special gifts.

Father Rose realized that the work had to become indigenous if the Philippine Church was to become the Church of the people. It was to the task of effecting that transition that he had addressed himself on his furlough, and it was why he had recruited me to set up a seminary for the training of a native priesthood.

When I told my parents that I had decided to surrender my fellowship in order to go to the Philippines, they were appalled. "The Philippines? Why, Clifford, that's on the other side of the world. Why don't you go to Kansas?"

So now, after weeks of building crates in which to pack my library and hurrying around New York to buy the clothing and other articles recommended by the people at the Church House, I found myself sitting on the rounded top of a bollard on the fantail deck of a ship plowing through the calm island waters between Seattle and Victoria, reviewing the momentous happenings of the past few months.

I had learned a good deal during my week in the reading room of the library. The word Igorot is derived from the native dialect and roughly means "man of the mountains." These men of the mountains were a fiercely independent primitive people dwelling in the Cordillera Central mountains of Northern Luzon. Until a few years before my arrival they had been feared as headhunters, and in the more remote parts of the mountains there were scattered groups of Igorots who still carried on this practice.

The Igorots are descendants of immigrants from the mainland of Asia who, in prehistoric times, had invaded the Philippine

13

archipelago looking for a new homeland. Like most Malayan people, their staple was rice, so they sought a place where there was abundant rainfall, flat land, and the heat needed for rice to thrive.

Reaching the Philippines, they found there the nomadic Aeta people, wandering around the fertile lowlands of Luzon. These were a timid negrito pygmy people, no match for the invaders who quickly expelled them from their lands. During the next few centuries other Malayan tribes, in even greater numbers than the ancestors of the Igorots, reached the Islands. They were the progenitors of the Tagalogs, Ilocanos, Visayans, Bicolanos, Pangasinenses, and other lowland groups who today make up the vast majority of the Filipino population. Probably the last to arrive were the Moros, who had already acquired their Muslim religion before leaving their ancestral homelands. The Igorots, finding that they could not stand against the hordes of later arrivals, gradually withdrew from the lowlands into the mountains of northern Luzon.

Here they found few level fields which they could convert into rice paddies, so they set to work reshaping the landscape. Scholars believe that the magnificent rice paddies in the neighborhood of Banaue were as much as five thousand years in construction. These estimates take into account the primitive tools employed and the numerous interruptions due to intertribal warfare.

The Banaue terraces are world famous. They extend from the floor of the valley up to the mountains, which they encircle, to a height of five thousand feet. It has been estimated that as much stone was used in the terrace walls as was used in all the pyramids of Egypt, and that the walls of individual terraces, if laid end to end, would reach around the world.

The Igorots, after building arable fields, found little need to defend them against intruders. Their innate suspicion of outsiders, and their reputation as "head-snatchers," as the Dutch in Borneo quaintly termed the Malayans of New Guinea and Borneo, who sprang from the same stock as the Igorots, gave them their longed-for privacy and freedom from incursions into the high ground which they had staked out as their own. Although the redoubtable Spanish conquistadores had made a fairly thorough sweep of the archipelago, they hadn't dared penetrate too far into the remote areas of the Cordillera Central. Even the Spanish Roman Catholic padres, members of the Augustinian order, were unwilling to venture too far into the mountains. Their work was chiefly a chaplaincy for the Spanish soldiers and government employees. Then, after America gained sovereignty over the Islands, as a result of the successful suppression in 1902 of the insurrection which had been led by General Aguinaldo, the Augustinians withdrew from the land of the Igorots.

The Vatican called upon non-Hispanic religious orders to

volunteer to fill the void created by the withdrawal of the Spaniards, and a Belgian order, the Congregation of the Immaculate Heart of Mary, centered in Brussels and Schuet, responded. By Christmas of 1907, eight members of this order, commonly known as "the Belgian Fathers," arrived to replace the Augustinians. Within five years this small band had increased to 40.

But since under the wise leadership of Bishop Charles Brent, Episcopal missionaries had adapted the policy of not proselytizing Roman Catholics, and of confining their missionary zeal to the non-Christian people, the Romans were tolerant of the presence of Episcopal missionaries in the area.

In only a few villages were Romans and Anglicans both at work among the Igorots. And even in these, there seemed to exist an unspoken agreement that neither group would interfere with the work of the other.

The Philippine government back in the 1930's estimated the "primitive population" of the area in question at something under half a million people, divided into at least a half dozen mutually hostile tribes, including Lepanto Igorots, Ifugaos, Bontocs, Kalingas, Apayaos, and Ilongots. In the census bureau's terminology, these were all classified as "primitive pagans." However, missionaries who lived among them smiled at the ignorance of those who thus characterized them. The Church at Sagada was crowded every Sunday with hundreds of "primitive pagans."

Our missionary teachers had educated hundreds of native children and knew that, given the education and the opportunity, they were capable of holding their own with anyone. There were Igorot nurses, teachers, and even a fully trained medical doctor who had been schooled in Canada and Manila. And now I was on my way to the Islands to help some of them become clergymen.

Father Rose had recruited another young man to return with him. He was Ezra Diman, just out of college, and he would replace the retiring headmaster of the high school in Sagada and become the supervisor of the dozen or so primary and intermediate schools located in our outstations. Father Rose, Diman and I had met in Seattle and had boarded the ship together.

Now that we were well under way with the complicated business of getting out of the harbor behind us, I thought it time to mingle with the other passengers. There were only 19 of us aboard. Two were executives of the Standard Oil Company, returning to their posts in China after furlough in the States. Later I visited one of these "old China hands" at his home in Shanghai and he told me that the green young deacon aboard the *President Madison* had stars in his eyes all the way across the Pacific, much to the amusement of the other passengers.

15

This gentleman had seen many young men making their first trip to Asia, and he seemed to think it was his duty to diminish their enthusiasm. He generally tried to show that a job is a job, wherever it is performed, and it is usually done more efficiently if the person doing it has been purged of all nonsensical notions of a mysterious, romantic and exotic Orient. I, however, being a clergyman, was a bit out of his line. He seemed a little puzzled about the course to be pursued in quenching the ardor of this newly hatched missionary.

Several days out, during which we had engaged in numerous conversations about national and international affairs, about current and past literature, and other trivia, he dove into the heart of the matter which he had been trying to introduce for several days.

"God doesn't care whether a man is a Buddhist, or a Christian, a Jew or a pagan," began the standard argument he had decided to employ in baiting me, "so why do you? Those chaps up in the hills of Luzon are perfectly happy. They don't need the worries you'll give them if you go interfering with their simple religion. Why don't you leave them alone?"

One must live among pagans, day in and day out, over a long period of time, in order to appreciate the falsity of the glib argument my friend had voiced. It was only after being with the Igorots for years that I became convinced that there is no such thing as a "carefree and happy pagan." Years more of living with other primitive heathen people in Ovamboland, Southwest Africa, have confirmed my conviction that the "carefree pagan" is a myth. He is too filled with anxiety about the future, with dread of the supernatural and the unknown. Because of these fears he is so likely to fall victim to any new "ism" that comes along that he cannot have that peace of mind which is necessary to true happiness.

But at that time I was only recently out of seminary, and while I felt sure that I was very close to being omniscient in all matters pertaining to theology, I still had enough sense to realize that I did not know enough about Igorot culture and religion to be able to dispute the thesis so easily stated.

Because I did not have a ready response to his objection to my choice of career my shipboard friend seemed to think that his question had stymied me. So we didn't talk religion any more. Instead, we played bridge all the way to Japan. It was only as we neared Shanghai that he reopened the subject from an entirely different angle.

"How much salary will you be getting?" I told him that not counting the value of housing, medical care and other fringe benefits such as travel and long furloughs, I would be getting approximately a hundred dollars a month. The oil company executive gasped and said, "If that was all I could get on ¡payday,¡ I'd run off and hide in the mountains, too." A couple of years later when I was his house-guest in Shanghai he offered to find me a job in the commercial

16

world, and when I told him that I had never expected to grow rich in the service of God and that my pittance was sufficient for my needs he shook his head gravely and said, "Cliff, you are hopeless."

The days on shipboard passed quickly. We made brief calls at Yokohama, Shanghai, and Hong Kong. The port calls gave us an opportunity to bargain for custom-made cotton and linen suits, for rainwear at fantastically low prices and for curios to send home. We were also able to become acquainted with the delicious cuisine of the Far East.

About three weeks after leaving the States we arrived in Manila, a city steaming in 100° heat and 95% humidity. The cooling rains were still several months ahead. Relief for us, we were told by our genial host, Bishop Gouverneur Frank Mosher, lay only two days away at the 5000-foot altitude of Sagada, so we lost no time arranging to get there.

In the closing months of the Second World War, in their pursuit of General Yamashita, the "Tiger of Malaya," and his defeated army, the American soldiers turned Philippine mountain footpaths into jeep trails and horse trails into highways. They built bridges across deep chasms. They laid airstrips in hitherto inaccessible parts of the province. The soldiers eventually left, but the improvements remained. Today the traveler can make the trip from Manila into the interior with very little inconvenience.

But in December 1931, it was an altogether different matter. We started our journey by taking a train to the railhead in La Union Province. By pre-arrangement we were met by Baldo, an Ilocano who had a good car and who was always available for the Mountain Province missionaries. We were driven to Tagudin, a barrio on the shores of Lingayen Gulf. The Mission maintained a rest house there. This was shaded by palm trees, and was situated just above the high tide mark on the beach of the China Sea. It was an idyllic place for short rests.

We learned to look forward to stopovers at the rest house. A meal there was always a delight. There was usually "Tagudin soup," as we called it. This was a thin broth, highly flavored with wood-smoke, pepper, and an assortment of indistinguishable but exquisite flavors left over from scores of meals previously cooked in the same clay pot. Next, the daughter of the caretaker would offer us "meat of the pig" with hearty assurances that we need not be afraid to eat it, for this pig, "she was clean, I know his mother. We fed her ourselves with only clean garbage, and our toilet does not empty into his pen, so don't be afraid of the meat of this pig." She often had "meat of the chicken" on the menu also, and frequently there was a side dish of fish freshly caught from the Gulf.

After a night's rest in Tagudin, we boarded a bus and proceeded into the mountains by way of Cervantes in Ilocos Sur. In those days travelling on a provincial bus for any distance required a sense of humor, a well padded fundament, and above all, patience. The vehicles were open with wooden bench seats across their width. As in most countries of Asia, the passenger was permitted to carry as much baggage and freight, animate and inanimate, as he could find room for in, on top of, or dangling outside the bus. So crates of chickens, cans of paint, sheets of galvanized iron roofing, sacks of grain, trussed-up squealing pigs, frightened, crying children, and odd bits of personal luggage were stowed with casual carelessness wherever a bit of space might permit.

Since there were no properly equipped stations along the route, the driver would occasionally bring his contraption to a jarring halt and cheerfully sing out, "Here is where we wash our hands! Gentlemen on the left side of the road, and señoras behind the bushes on the right." And, if there were any nuns aboard, "Please to let the madres go first."

Motion sickness afflicted most of the passengers. The well advised traveller would wear a handkerchief over his nose and mouth to exclude the noxious smells and also to keep from choking in the clouds of dust swirling from the unpaved roads.

Despite the discomfort, and because of the beauty of the country, the ride into the Mountain Province in those pre-war days could still be an enjoyable and memorable experience.

The first adventure usually consisted of the crossing of the Amburayan River. In the dry season this simply meant holding fast to the bench in front of your own while the bus bounced for several hundred yards over the wide rocky stream bed. The passenger had to be ready, at the request of the driver, to dismount and help him roll away any large boulders that might be lying in the path of the bus. If the trip was being made after the monsoon rains had begun, however, the transit of the Amburayan became downright dangerous.

In the rainy season the river swelled to a torrent, roaring along through several channels. The widest and most turbulent of these had to be crossed on a bamboo raft which was loosely attached to a cable strung aloft. Often the raft was so heavily laden that the muddy waters washed the floors of the cars it carried. Lest the current suddenly swing the raft around and dump everything into the rushing stream, huge stones were employed to chock the wheels of each vehicle.

Soon after crossing the river, the road began its climb into the foothills of the Cordillera Central mountains, that rugged mass of tumbled hills which forms the spine of Northern Luzon. Deeper into the mountains, the road narrowed to a single lane. This unpaved road was scratched out of the sides of precipitous dirt slopes or chiselled out of cliffs of solid rock.

In places it hung precariously a hundred feet above a valley densely matted with jungle flora. One got the fearful impression that if the lane were inches narrower, the outer wheels of the car would have nothing more substantial than humid tropical air on which to roll. As the road pushed farther into the mountains, it gained altitude by making innumerable hairpin turns on frightfully steep grades. From high places one could look back and see this snake-like trail writhing through the jungle.

In later years I was to hear the tale of how a certain section of the road came to be built. An American contractor had decided to employ Igorot labor as much as possible. He therefore sent a message to a village near the route of the proposed road and invited interested Igorots to bid for the rough work of excavating a hillock that lay athwart the route.

In response, a frail old man appeared at his camp and said that he had looked over the site and would like to take the job. His price would be two cases of canned fish and a few hands of tobacco leaf. The American, figuring that he couldn't lose much on such a contract, even if the results were poor, awarded the job to the old man.

After several days, concerned at having seen no gang of laborers going to the hill, the American decided to investigate. Reaching the site, he saw his sub-contractor sitting on top of the hill he had agreed to remove, puffing on his little brass pipe and speculatively eyeing the passing clouds.

"Why no work?" demanded the contractor. The old Igorot pointed to a few ditches he had scratched out of the hill and said, "See? I work."

In a mixture of Spanish, Ilocano and English, and with much arm waving, the American ranted against his squatting partner. "You call that work? Must remove whole hill. Need many men, many shovels. Must finish soon. Go get some men to help you!"

The imperturbable old man merely puffed on his pipe, squinted at the sky, and replied, "You see. Soon hill gone. Before evening, you see."

Realizing that he could do no more, the contractor threw a few more insults at the patriarch and started back to his camp, resolved to find someone the next day who would take the job seriously. Before he could reach the shelter of his hut, a heavy rain began and he soon heard the unmistakable sound of a massive landslide from the direction whence he had come. He retraced his steps and reached what had been the hill. There he saw the old man proudly surveying a shapeless mound of mud and rock lying in the river canyon.

Little remained to be done but to clean up the fringes. The force of water rushing through a few judiciously placed ditches had completed in a few minutes what scores of men would have taken days to accomplish.

Of such native ingenuity I knew nothing on that first bus trip into the mountains. I was then concerned with the vital task of holding onto the bench in front of me to keep from being bounced out of the jolting vehicle.

More than once, our driver who had so cheerfully accepted much more freight and many more passengers than was either safe or practical, stopped at the foot of long grades and asked the passengers to help him unload car-sick pigs and indignant chickens, as well as much of the heavy luggage. All hands joined in carrying the baggage up the hill while he coaxed his bus, lightened considerably, up the steep grade. At the top we reloaded and clambered aboard to enjoy a few more kilometers of breath-taking, and heart-stopping mountain scenery.

Someone, in describing the Philippine mountain roads as they were before World War II, said that if one listened closely he could hear the whir of angels' wings as they flitted by.

Especially startling on the road from Ilocos Sur into the Mountain Province was the abrupt transition from tropical rain forest, which covered the western slope of the range, to the pine-covered steeps on the arid eastern side. The road wound through jungle growth where fern trees, bamboos, and other flora typical of the steamy tropics, grew luxuriantly. Then the bus reached the pass—the saddleback at the top of the range. The road ran flat for perhaps 50 yards and then, dramatically, the jungle ended and the mountains were covered by a coniferous forest.

As grimly as we had been pushing the benches in front of us, as though to help the old bus make its groaning climb, now with one accord we pulled hard against them as though to slow our lurching descent to the town of Cervantes, baking at the bottom of this dry valley. Beyond Cervantes we entered Igorot country. We could see their villages, consisting of peaked grass-thatched huts, surrounded by tiny patches of corn, beans, tobacco and camotes, the native sweet potato. Next to each hut was a stone-walled sunken pigpen, with its tiny grass thatched hut at one end serving two purposes. It was a shelter for the occupant of the pen and it was also the toilet house for the residents of the hut.

When a car reached the gate, the gate-keeper would sing out a cheery greeting to the travellers and then crank the ancient telephone which hung on the wall of his shack. He shouted his report of the arrival of a car and asked his colleague at the next gate whether it was safe for his vehicle to proceed or whether some other car was on the road headed towards his gate. Often, as I listened to the gate-keepers bellow into the phone, I wondered why they muffled their voices by shouting into the instrument, when by merely facing the direction of the next gate and using the same lusty hollering they might easily be heard without it.

It was exasperating to wait, especially if the afternoon rains had begun, for one never knew when tons of mud and rock might fall from the overhanging mountain and block the road for hours, or even weeks. In spite of this primitive though effective system of traffic control, accidents did sometimes occur. In 1935 the Roman Catholics held an International Eucharistic Congress in Manila. One of the American priest-delegates had asked us whether he might visit us before returning to the States. I went down to Dontay, the closest point to Sagada that his bus would come, to meet him. He was a huge man, about 6'8", and fleshed out like a bull, but he was trembling like an aspen leaf in a summer breeze when he got off the bus.

He told me that they had been following another bus from Cervantes, but when they had reached the gate several kilometers back, they did not see it ahead of them. This could mean only one thing, so they had all run back looking over the side of the cliff as they ran. Then they saw the missing bus, nearly a hundred feet down in the canyon, smashed and still smouldering. Only a tiny baby out of the group of 32 passengers had survived.

A special source of annoyance on the single-lane roads was the travelling politician. To impress upon everybody his importance, he would have the gate-keepers for two gates ahead hold traffic so that he might speed through with a minimum of delay and a maximum of flair.

Only once was I accorded such a privilege. I was travelling in a station wagon from Baguio to Sagada, accompanying a casket containing the body of one of our staff members who had died of typhoid fever. I had made no request for special attention—I didn't have to. Word was phoned ahead all the way and either reverence for or fear of the dead assured me of a stop-free trip that day.

But this was all still far ahead of me. I had not yet reached Sagada for my first sight of where I would be living for several years to come. In the early thirties there was no direct bus service into Sagada, so we disembarked at Dontay and there transferred into a private car sent out by the Mission. It was late afternoon, some ten hours after having started from Tagudin, before we reached the Sagada gate.

When we got within a kilometer of Sagada, the road was lined on both sides by Igorot villagers and children from the Mission school. The men were clad only in g-strings, and the women in wrap-around hand-woven knee-length skirts, some of them with short blouses and some bare above the waist, and all lustily singing their welcome to our party in the unique harmonies of age-old Igorot chants. The men beat on brass *ganzas** and drums to provide rhythm for the singers.

---

*A ganza was a dish-like brass gong, hanging from a human jaw-bone, or, in later times, a wooden replica of a jaw-bone.

The car slowed almost to a halt as the villagers pressed in to shout their greeting to Father Rose and to the two new missionaries whom he had brought back with him. There was no mistaking the warmth of the welcome. They knew Father Rose loved them. Had he not left his own wife and daughter in the States to resume his ministry among them? Their boisterous welcome showed how glad they were that he had come back to them. They were his people—and I experienced the thrill of realizing that soon they would be mine, too. As I looked at the crowd of excited school boys I wondered how many of them would be offering themselves for training in the seminary I was there to establish. I didn't dream that a great war would soon engulf the Islands, and that it would advance our time-table so greatly that even now there were in that crowd at least half a dozen young men who would become priests, and two others who would also become bishops.

But my primary thought at the moment was that it had been a long trip from New York, and I had at last reached what was to be my home for the next six years. And I was very tired.

In the course of those six years I heard many visitors to our station express the same astonishment I felt that afternoon when I caught my first glimpse of the mission compound. After driving for hours through the countryside, where the only buildings were Igorot huts, one turned off the road into the mission property and there saw a huge stone church looming over everything. Except for the fact that a bell tower, surmounted by a huge wooden cross was at the front of this structure, one might have mistaken it for a fort. And that was how Father Staunton had designed it. A few years before there had been a dawn raid on Sagada by warriors from Bontoc, enemies of the Lepanto Igorots from time immemorial. This raid was carried out with such speed and stealth that many villagers had been killed before they were awake enough to know what was happening. Father Staunton wanted a building into which his people could flee in the event of another such occurrence. Fortunately, it never had to serve as a place of refuge. A few years later the elders of the Sagada and Bontoc tribes agreed to forget their enmity and live in peace.

It was into this church that we were led, followed by hundreds in the welcoming crowd. There we took part in a short service of thanksgiving for our safe arrival, with prayers that our ministry would be pleasing to God and beneficial to the people.

By this time dusk had fallen, so we proceeded to Father Rose's house for a wash-up and a sumptuous dinner.

Ezra Diman and I were assigned apartments in the Boys' School building to which we were happy to be escorted, happy also to see the end of this long and exhausting day.

I spent the next few days exploring my new home and becoming acquainted with my colleagues.

Sagada lay at the northern end of a long valley in which there were several other villages. It was divided into three parts. The missionary residences were built on hills on the northern and eastern perimeters of the valley. The *barrio*, at the northwest end of the valley was where the Filipino teachers, nurses and other employees of the mission lived. Many of these were Igorots, although some were Ilocanos who had been recruited from the lowlands before there had been enough Igorots sufficiently well trained to take over the tasks. The third division of the town was the *ili** where the majority of the Igorots lived in their grass-thatched huts.

An ili was made up of several neighborhoods, the boundaries of which were usually determined by the terrain. Each ili was served by the centrally located *dapay+* which was the social, political, religious and cultural center. It consisted of a small open area, paved with flat stones, with a space thereon in which a small fire might burn. It was there that some of the sacrifices to the *anitos[o]* might be offered. At one end of the dapay there was a long low hut, which served as the dormitory for adolescent boys and men who were not living in families. In this central meeting place the men of the neighborhood would meet to set the dates for planting and harvest festivals. Here, too, would be decided how to deal with various problems of the neighborhood families. This often meant that those wise in the art would be consulted to see if an identification of the anito responsible for the misfortune could be made and what type of sacrifice might be necessary to placate the disgruntled spirit.

---

ili, a village or small group of houses.
+*dapay.* the meeting place for a neighborhood.
[o]*anito,* supernatural spirit. (See pp. 28-29 for fuller explanation.)

CHAPTER II

These brief exploratory trips, with potential seminary students as my guides, made it very clear to me that I had to learn more about the ways and beliefs of the people from whom they came before I could set up classes. The station ministered to a vast area and Father Rose needed the services of another clergyman, so it was arranged that I would assist him in the routine evangelical and pastoral work and then, when I felt sufficiently acquainted with the people, get on with the task of organizing the seminary.

Father Rose assured me that I would best learn by getting out among the people. He was a wise teacher. He knew that most young clergymen imagine themselves next only to God in wisdom, and that it would be a waste of time trying to tell me how to proceed. I would have to make my own mistakes and, hopefully, profit thereby.

I set out one day with my interpreter to a village where we had an outstation. We rode our horses to Bagnen and then clambered over the top of the mountain and descended to Data on foot. This was a village of about 200 souls where the Christian community was very small and where many of the pagan leaders were opposed to the extension of Christian influence.

I know now that it was out of curiosity, although at the time I probably thought it a personal tribute to me, that a large group of village elders had gathered in the central dapay. They were there to see the new *Apo Padi** who had come from America to live in Sagada. After a few preliminary words by way of self introduction, I launched into my talk with Genesis 1:1 and painstakingly progressed through the whole saga of God's dealings with men as outlined in the Pentateuch. After I had brought the tribes of Israel out of Egypt and into the Holy Land, I told them of God's continued concern for them as shown in the ministry of the prophets. I did not ignore the rise and fall of the United Kingdom, nor the history of the separated kingdoms of Israel and Judah. I may have missed a few of the less important events of those centuries, but if I did, it was by oversight.

Before I had got well into the arrival of Jesus on the scene, my large audience had dwindled considerably, first one bored listener

---

*Apo is an honorific which might be translated as "reverend" or "honorable." It would often be untranslatable but it could be said that the person so designated was worthy of respect. "Padi" was the Igorot contraction of "padre."

and then another quietly sneaking off. By the time I had reached the crucifixion and the resurrection only a few remained. Still, I was flattered and touched by their apparent interest and devotion until I learned that they were residents of the dormitory attached to that dapay where we were meeting, and had no other place to go.

"Well," I asked my interpreter, as we hiked back to Bagnen to get our horses, "how do you think it went?"

Gently and with genuine compassion, he replied, "Perhaps, Apo Padi, you tried to give them a little too much for one session. They are not very smart, you know."

The next time out I decided to let the people set the course of the session, so I invited questions and comments.

"I shall never become a Christian," declared one wrinkled old man emphatically.

"Why?"

"Because Jesus was not fair," he replied. "Why was He born among the Americans and not among us Igorots? Are we not as good as you are?"

"But He did not come among the Americans," I explained patiently. "He was born in the land of the Jews long ago because they and only they among all the people of the world at that time knew anything about the one true God. In that way He was able to start with people who were already fairly well prepared, and work from that point, whereas if he had come among the ancestors of the Americans or the Igorots He would have had to spend a long time convincing them first that there is but one God."

"That may be," admitted my stubborn inquisitor, "but He still was not fair."

"Why?"

"Well, people then and there could see Him and talk to Him. They had a chance to seek His help for their problems. But He has left us now without that help."

"Oh, no, my friend," I remonstrated, "if that were so, I would agree that He is unfair. But all during the time He was with the Jews, He knew that soon He would be killed by His enemies, so He was preparing his friends to carry on His work. Then He was executed. But He won over death by rising again, showing us once and for all that the love of God cannot be destroyed by the evil of men. After He rose from the dead, He told us that He would forever be among us, even until the end of the world."

"But He isn't, is He?" countered the Igorot with an air of triumphant finality.

"Ah, but He is," I said with equal certainty. "He sent his Holy Spirit to remain with us, to lead us through perplexities and troubles, and to show us the sure way to God. And He arranged that men would always be able to come into His presence, whenever they choose to, in the service we call Holy Communion, and to receive the same strength and help which He gave His friends during His time on earth. So, my friend, from the earliest days of Christianity down to the present time, in every land, among every kind of people, His followers may find Him on countless altars throughout the world. Only in His physical body has He left us."

I wish I could say that this dialogue resulted in an immediate convert, but I don't think that's what happened. I do know, however, that at least the old Igorot left our meeting looking very thoughtful.

"You are learning," was the only comment my interpreter made as we turned homeward that afternoon. He was Edward Longid, my language teacher and a student in my embryonic seminary. Edward was my constant companion on the visits I made to my outstations. He was a gentle lad, a person of keen intelligence and of a humble heart, and I was very proud a few years later when he was ordained to the priesthood.

Often our first opportunity to bring the Gospel to people is through ministry to the mind or body. Accordingly, we established primary schools in as many places as we had chapels. In the central station our educational system went through the grades and into high school. Both boys and girls were encouraged to go as far as their ability would allow.

We were convinced that the Igorot could and should take his place in the world of the twentieth century. Time had passed him by and he had been scorned and exploited by men who were in no way superior in intelligence, but who, through accidents of history, had been given opportunities denied the Igorot.

We were also convinced that people value that which comes to them at a price more than that which is free, so our boys and girls had to pay small fees for their schooling and board. Sometimes this consisted of one or two eggs a week, which the missionaries would buy and which often turned out to be a bad bargain for the purchaser because the Igorot liked his eggs rather ripe. (In fact, a favorite native delicacy is the *balut*, a boiled half-hatched duck egg.) More often the fee would be a few centavos which could be paid in produce. The boys and girls who lived in the dormitories paid higher fees than the day pupils, and also were expected to perform some service for the common good, such as gardening or weaving or lace-making. The missionaries employed as many of the school children as they could afford. I had one little youngster, now a priest, whose sole duty was to keep a record of the rainfall on charts I furnished him.

We knew that we had to educate our children because primitive man is a creature of fear. Only as he is educated and learns to master his environment does he cease to cringe at the awesome manifesta-

26

tions of nature's power. To go from fear of natural forces to confident mastery of his surroundings depends upon man's understanding of the workings of nature. From a desk in a primary school to a ride in a lunar buggy is a natural progression and our task was to start it. So primarily schools were the important first step.

This was especially so in this society where women had been regarded as little more than drones or breeding mares. The men did the heavy work, to be sure, but this was seasonal or occasional. The women worked all day long, and were expected as well to carry on all household tasks. It was the women who planted, after the men had driven the water buffalo hitched to the plough through the mud of the rice paddy. It was the women who weeded. It was the women who harvested, helped only occasionally by the men, and it was the women who winnowed and threshed the grain.

Some Igorot families disliked sending their girls to the mission school because they feared that we would spoil them by giving them the idea that it was degrading to soil one's clothes in a muddy rice field. But when we began producing graduates of the schools who could go on to become teachers or registered nurses, this opposition to the education of their girls vanished. One of our missionaries, Deaconess Evelyn Ashcroft, had enormous success in founding a school for the training of *catechistas*, girls who had a thoroughly sound religious training and who were competent to go into the villages to train teachers in the methodology of religious pedagogy. They often prepared classes for confirmation, and their assistance to the overworked clergy cannot be too highly praised.

If a religion is to become indigenous to a region, it must be led by the sons and daughters of that region. Our goal was to educate Igorots to become teachers, catechists, nurses and priests. Through our medical ministry, too, we opened the hearts of many to the love of God. Our first resident American doctor was Hawkins Jenkins, a gentle and well trained physician, a native of South Carolina.

The people living in the immediate environs of Sagada, where we had a dispensary ever since the establishment of the Mission in 1905, had learned the value of western medicine, but it was more difficult to carry this knowledge to the sick folk of the outstations. Sometimes we tried to introduce our medical ministry to them by taking along with us on our outstation trips a trained dispensary attendant or a nurse. On rare occasions when duties of the central hospital permitted, the doctor would accompany us. But there was risk in this practice, for there could be no follow-up unless we could persuade the sick person to go into Sagada.

We had learned, too, that it is not always safe to leave strong medicine with sick folk removed from close medical supervision. Too often we found that when a patient was told that one pill thrice a day would bring relief he figured that two pills as often would work twice as fast.

In visiting the outstations, I naturally kept my eyes open for cases of illness for which hospitalization was imperative. One day, while visiting in Bila, I was told that the people had isolated an old man because he was suffering from *na-kilot* (dirtiness). The secondary meaning of the word was unknown to me at the time, so I went to the outskirts of the village where the old man had been housed in an abandoned rice granary. Tenderly, I prodded the suppurating sores on his skin and tried to get all the information I could about the course of his illness that I might describe the case in detail to our doctor in Sagada. When I had completed the examination, I washed well in the stream nearby.

My ablutions were far more vigorous and thorough the next day when the doctor told me that my patient was probably suffering from leprosy. Though instances of this disease were rare in the Igorot country, the law required that we report such cases as we might discover to the provincial health authorities. Then they had to apprehend the ill person and send him or her off to the insular leprosarium at Culion, an island far to the south. Knowing this, when the villagers suspected that there was a case of na-kilot among them, in compassion they would try to hide the unfortunate victim so that he need not leave his or her family and friends and the bracing air of the high mountains for the humidity, heat, and loneliness of Culion.

As Chaplain of our hospital in Sagada, I often donned an operating gown and mask and watched the surgical procedures. I even assisted in minor ways. I did this primarily because the Igorot, so thoroughly indoctrinated in the belief that there is a connection between health and religion, felt a little more reassured when submitting to surgery if he knew that his pastor was near at hand.

For several years, before St. Theodore's Hospital in Sagada was structurally complete, we had to get by with makeshift facilities. The room for the chapel had not yet been constructed, so we set up an altar at the end of one of the corridors. The Igorot, as new as he was to Christianity, would have been most puzzled had he come into an institution of healing which did not proclaim the concern of God for those who were ill.

Even pagan patients who had agreed reluctantly to try "Christian medicine" were not deprived of spiritual help to their liking in St. Theodore's. We often found that their family members who had come ostensibly to visit had actually come to aid in the healing process. They brought a few live chickens, and seeking out a secluded spot near the hospital, they would squat and sacrificially offer the fowl to the anito responsible for the illness.

Anito is a generic name for any supernatural spirit of which there are thousands, perhaps millions. Some are the souls of people who once lived. Some are the spirits of natural forces, like storms, the sun, the moon, the stars, etc. Others are spirits which inhabit the streams, the fields, trees, and particular places in the environment. The word was also used to describe the upright posts and stones crudely shaped like a human figure, which were to be seen in the dapays. These were thought to have magical properties and sacrifices were offered to them.

The anitos are interested in the everyday life of human beings. They are benevolent or malevolent depending upon their whims and whether or not they have received the respectful attention of the people, shown by the offering of animal sacrifice or small gifts of food or tobacco.

The pagan Igorot had a simple explanation for any misfortune which he could not attribute to the direct act of another person or animal. Whether these were individual instances of bad luck, like a leak in the walls of the rice fields, a fire, accident or disease, or whether they were situations arising from some great natural calamity, like an earthquake or a typhoon, the anitos were blamed.

It then became the task of those who were skilled in reading signs or those who could interpret dreams, to discover which among the multitude of spirits was causing the trouble. The proper sacrifices would then be offered. It might be that the anito could be placated by the sacrifice of a single chicken. In more extreme cases, the offering of a big animal, like a pig, or even a water buffalo, might be necessary before the evil could be remedied. If the misfortune did not cease, it was not because the spirits had not caused it, but rather because insufficient sacrifice had been offered or because the proper anito had not been identified and placated.

Most Igorots, Christian and pagan alike, had great respect for all the good Christianity had accomplished among the people, even though in numerous instances the pagan Igorot maintained that he himself was too old to change his beliefs and customs.

Once I was visiting a village in which we were just starting work, so we did not as yet have a chapel. I asked where I might set up an altar, which in this case was to be merely a few planks resting on rocks. I was told that I might use the "sacred grove." So, in good faith, I did, not knowing that the Igorot who had given me permission was a Christian who had spoken without clearing it with the village elders, all of whom were devoutly pagan.

When the service was over, my catechist told me that there was an indignation meeting going on at the end of the grove, led by a very hostile pagan.

"The American Padi has done a wicked thing in offering sacrifice in our sacred grove," said the old man.

"But do we not regard this grove as sacred because we ourselves have made it so by offering our own sacrifices therein?" asked another pagan leader.

Receiving nods of agreement from other participants of the meeting, he continued. "Then if our sacrifices can make holy that which was merely a place among the trees before, think, brothers, will not the offering of the Christian sacrifice to the Christian God make it doubly holy?"

"Yes, perhaps," agreed the original speaker, "but it is dangerous, for we will never really know until the anitos send misfortune or good luck to show us how they feel."

In the end, I was not asked to remove the altar, and there it stayed until our chapel was completed.

This little episode illustrates just how fatalistic the pagan Igorot philosophy was. The pagan accepted whatever came as the will of the spirits, even though his grandchild with only the beginning of a primary education might see that some natural cause lay behind a calamity which was mysterious in origin to the pagan.

There was a fatal slide at Balugan, for example.

Suyo, a small village on the east side of this valley south of Sagada, was one of my outstations. Going there early one morning I rode through a dense fog. A typhoon in the area had brought torrential rain which had lasted for several days, but now only the fog remained. When I reached Suyo I was dismayed to find only one crippled old man in the chapel. "Where is everyone?" I asked.

"They are all up at Balugan trying to help. We heard a giant roar this morning, just before sunrise, and soon thereafter, Letdug, from Balugan, came down to Suyo and told us that there had been a bad slide, and that many houses had been buried, and many people killed."

Almost before he had finished speaking, I was back in my saddle and hurrying toward Balugan as fast as the tired animal would take me.

The disaster was far worse than I had anticipated. The whole face of a mountain, towering 400 feet above the village, had collapsed and buried what must have been about three score houses beneath it.

The first slide, a comparatively small one, had occurred in the middle of the night, and in response to the screams of the people entrapped in the houses in the path of the slide, the men of the village had rushed in to help. It was dark and foggy, and no one gave thought to the imminent danger of another slide. But as the rescuers worked, another avalanche of mud and rocks fell, following the course of the first slide, but gouging out a much wider path as it roared down the slope.

This second fall covered not only the originally stricken huts, but 20 or 30 more. Practically all of the men who had been at work trying to extricate their neighbors were themselves buried alive.

Under the low clouds we were now desperately digging, using crow bars, branches and a few spades, but for the most part only our hands. In the meanwhile I had sent word back to Sagada for Dr. Jenkins and his dispensary staff to hasten out, and the messenger had spread the alarm along the way with the result that throngs of volunteers were now appearing, equipped with more adequate tools for the task which lay before us.

As it turned out, the doctor had few patients to treat. Almost everyone in the path of the slide had been buried, and the only ones requiring medical attention were a few people who had skidded about in the sea of mud which had been a mountain. We were not able to uncover a single house and we quickly realized that even had we been able to dig faster, the residents would have been crushed or smothered to death.

No one was ever able to give an accurate figure of the casualties, for no one knew how many people may have been visiting in the houses which had been covered. The best guess was that the dead numbered between 100 and 130 although in the course of the next few days less than a dozen bodies were actually recovered.

By the time we had ceased our frantic efforts, which had failed to effect a single rescue, the fog had dissipated completely. We looked up at the overhanging mountain and we could see that here and there rocks and mud were still moving. Some of us scrambled up a back trail to reach the plateau atop the cliff to try to determine whether there might be danger of further slides.

What we saw was not reassuring. For perhaps 500 yards along the top of the cliff, from a few feet to 20 yards back from the edge of the newly created precipice, there was a great crack. It ranged in width from a few inches to several yards. It certainly appeared to us that more slides could be expected momentarily. I know that I trod lightly as I inspected the dangerous area.

For the remainder of the day, the Igorots who had accompanied me on the inspection and I tried to persuade the village elders to set an example by abandoning their houses and relocating elsewhere in a safer area. But the elders, stunned at the loss of so many of their people, were deaf to our plea. The anito had caused the slide, and all that would be necessary now would be to determine which spirits were at fault and what sort of sacrifice had to be offered.

I went down to Bontoc, the provincial capital, and tried to enlist the aid of the officials in commanding a general evacuation of what I thought was a doomed village. I failed. No one in the government thought his authority was sufficient for such an order.

I went to Manila. Since President **Manuel** Quezon was on one of his frequent visits to Washington seeking early legislation for the complete independence of the Philippines, I brought the case to the attention of Vice-President Sergio Osmeña.

Mr. Osmeña was both sympathetic and **cooperative.** "We do not hear promptly enough of these provincial tragedies down here in

Manila," he said, "but I shall telegraph at once for full details. In the meantime, Father Nobes, what can I do to help?"

I told him that we wanted three things. First, an order for the evacuation of Balugan, to be enforced by the Philippine Constabulary; second, an appropriation of two hundred pesos for each family thus evacuated; and finally, the allocation of another piece of land on which the new Balugan might be built. The Philippine Legislature was in session at the time, so relief legislation was rushed through, but in a rather different form from what I had hoped for. The Insular Government merely urged, and did not command, evacuation, and offered a bonus of fifty pesos to any householder who would leave his home and rebuild elsewhere, on a site he would have to acquire himself.

I returned to the Mountain Province and at a mass meeting explained what had been accomplished. What I said did not make me popular.

"We have sacrificed," remonstrated the old men. "Nothing more will happen to the village. You speak of cracks in the cliff. We, too, have looked at them. The anito will protect us and forbid the earth to move again if we continue to do them honor. But if we leave our homes, the spirits will be angry with us for our lack of trust and will pursue us with misfortune wherever we may go."

In spite of this warning, several dozen families did leave their homes, just long enough to apply for the bonus of fifty pesos. After a few months, they were all back in Balugan, under the shadow of the man-killing mountain. They were quite happy in their belief that the spirits had been placated and that nothing more would happen to them.

Now, more than 50 years after that tragic day, still nothing has happened. The scar on the mountainside has been grown over. The tons of debris which snuffed out the lives of so many in a few heart-stopping minutes now form fertile fields for the cultivation of corn, beans and tobacco.

They were right and I was wrong. Perhaps the local seers located the proper anito the first time around. Or perhaps the numerous prayers the hundreds of Christians of the region offered for the safety of the people of Balugan were the effective factors. Only God knows the answer.

CHAPTER III

The school which started in my living room with a student body of three, two of whom later became bishops of thriving dioceses within the Republic of the Philippines, has since grown to become St. Andrew's Theological Seminary, now in Quezon City, just outside of Manila, the largest Episcopal seminary outside of the United States, with students from all of Southeast Asia.

In 1932 we had few candidates for the ministry. While I was on furlough several years later people would sometimes ask me what chair I occupied in the Seminary, and I told them that it was not a chair, but a bench, for I taught Old Testament, New Testament, Church History, Doctrine, Moral Theology and Ethics, Canon Law, Apologetics, Homiletics, Liturgics, Religious Education and Parish Administration.

It was very bewildering for young men passing from the simplicity of their tribal culture into the sophistication of the twentieth century. One of my houseboys told me one day, quite seriously, that he was not sure whether he would become a priest or a plumber. Both occupations were from a different civilization. Both were therefore equally attractive for one who was turning his back on the primitive culture of his forefathers, and the duties of each fascinated him. He eventually became a priest.

Since there was not enough teaching work to occupy all of my time in those early years in Sagada, I spent a lot of time ministering to some of the outstation congregations.

Naturally I was trying hard to become proficient in the dialect of the region. It is a Malayan, agglutinative language. Early missionaries had been content to use Ilocano, one of the major languages of the lowland Filipinos which was used extensively throughout Central and Northern Luzon. There was a tendency among some of the Igorots to use Ilocano in an attempt to disguise their tribal affiliation. We worked hard to discourage this feeling that being an Igorot was a cause for shame. We pointed out to them that they had never been subservient to any other race, that the very name Igorot usually inspired fear in other Filipinos. We told them to be proud of their heritage, to use their own dialect, and to continue following their ancestral ways in every way that was not incompatible with their Christian religion.

Actually, it would have been much simpler to use Ilocano. There was an extensive literature, including the Bible, in this lowland dialect, and recognized grammars and dictionaries were available. Igorot was something else again. The Lepanto Igorot dialect, in use around Sagada, had not been reduced to writing except in a few mission publications such as simple catechisms and prayer forms. One had to learn the nuances and meanings of words by using them. But, like most dialects of primitive people, the language had a simple basic structure, so after a few weeks of absorbing the rules of grammar and then by diligently practicing conversation, one soon became facile in the language.

Because religion was my primary concern I was disappointed to find that while Igorot was wealthy in concrete terms, it was woefully deficient in words expressing abstract ideas. This, too, is a characteristic of most primitive languages.

For instance, there were a dozen words for "basket," depending upon the size, the use to which it was put, the material of which it was made, and even its color. However, there was only one word, *nemnem*, to translate "thought," "idea," "will," "intention," "mind," "plan," "purpose" and even the organ whence emanated all of this, the "brain."

People who were not aware of this and who attempted to speak through interpreters would sometimes get into extravagant dilemmas. There was the visiting priest from China who sought to illustrate the vastness of God's creation by speaking of the universe in all its grandeur. He spoke of astronomical distances, using the term "light years." His interpreter bravely spoke of years "light in color," "light in weight," light in responsibility," but at length he realized that he was making no sense either of what he was hearing or of what he was saying. Pretending to translate the visitor's strange homily by pausing now and then as though to listen, he proceeded to preach a sermon of his own composition.

Another priest whose diction was not so good thought it appropriate in All Saints Church, Bontoc, to talk about the saints. He told his audience that they were before us for our encouragement and example, that we must love them, that we must thank God for them, and that only if we followed them would we find fellowship with God. Unfortunately the interpreter had missed the key word and blithely said all of these nice things about "sins." It was a baffled congregation that left the Church that day.

Bishop Mosher had served for years in the China Mission before he became second Bishop of the Philippines. While he was fluent in the Mandarin language of China, he never attempted to learn any of the numerous dialects spoken throughout the breadth of his jurisdiction in the Philippines. "If there isn't someone around who can understand English well enough to translate for me," he said to me

34

one day, "then our years of educational work among these people have been spent in vain and that I refuse to believe. Don't tell me I can't use English wherever I go in my Diocese, unless you want to make me angry." So I never mentioned it to him again. I did, however, quietly continue to pursue my study of Igorot.

The Igorot often fashions new words out of English words by adding Igorot prefixes and suffixes to them, even as we have anglicized words from other languages. One day a delegation of village elders waited upon the Bishop and with much dignity addressed him thus: "*Nen-meet-meet-meetingkami ya idwani menpetitionkami ken sika, Apo Obisbo* Mosher, *ta idyam isnan Apo* Governor General *nan petitionmi, gapu tay nan primo petitionmi wada isnan waste-basketna.*"

The Bishop looked puzzled for a moment, but as I started to translate for him, he said, "Now wait, Clifford, let me see if I've got this. They've had a lot of meetings and now they want me to take their petition to the Governor General because their first petition" . . . and he broke into loud laughter . . . "has ended up in the waste basket."

When he finally stopped laughing the Bishop said, "Tell them I quite understand their difficulty, and that I shall happily take the petition to the Governor and jolly well make sure that he reads it."

We tried to give our school children a good command of simple English. However, the school boy's most treasured volume was his dictionary, and he would spend hours poring over it trying to master all of the multi-syllabic words, and paying scant attention to those of Anglo-Saxon origin. He felt that this would prove that he was indeed well learned.

An American professor at the University of the Philippines told me about an experience he had had with his garden boy. There had been a particularly heavy rain. When it subsided the professor told the gardener to dig a ditch to permit the water to run off. The boy looked confused for a while, then trotted out to the garden to see what might be needing his attention. When my friend realized that the boy had not understood, he said again: "Dig a ditch and let the water drain off."

The boy still did not understand, so the American took a spade and starting digging.

"Oh, sir, I see," said the boy, "but why did you not tell me I was to excavate a drainage canal?"

Because of my desire to learn the dialect as quickly and thoroughly as I could, I tried as much as possible to work in the language independently of my assigned tutors. I often sat with old men in the dapay and let them laugh at me as I stumbled through a conversation with them.

One day after I had been in Sagada for a few months, I decided to precede my porter and my interpreter and to walk alone to Tadian, which was our destination. I had made the trip several times before but always with someone else.

Halfway through the forest that lies between Bagnen and Tadian, I came to a fork in the trail. I presumed that the path most worn would be the proper one, so I followed it, only to find myself on the bank of a stream which I had never seen before. Instead of retracting my steps to the fork in the trail, I foolishly cut through the shrubbery, thinking to intercept the other path.

I must have spent half an hour wandering in circles, climbing in and out of the unfamiliar stream. I was becoming more and more annoyed with myself, and not a little panicky. Whether it would be a hostile Igorot or an unfriendly python (neither of which existed within a radius of 50 miles of where I was thrashing about) I did not know, but I was beginning to fear that I might soon come to some sort of inglorious end.

It was with much relief that I heard the sound of a woodchopper not far off. I headed for it and came across a pretty young Igorot woman who had been delimbing a large pine tree. She was as startled as I at the unexpected encounter, but she didn't run away, and as she looked friendly enough, I opened the conversation.

My Igorot vocabulary was limited, but after thinking it through carefully, I managed to stutter, *"Ento nan daan ay omey id Tadian?"* (Where is the trail to Tadian?) The girl looked me over, made as though to speak, and then shrugged her shoulders expressively.

So I rearranged the words a little and tried again. She muttered: *"Adik ma-awatan,"* which even I knew meant "I don't understand." She turned back to her sticks as though the matter were finished.

But I persisted. With gestures, by drawing maps on the forest floor and by trying every possible arrangement of my few Igorot words, I kept trying to communicate, but it seemed to me as she stared blankly at me that I must have stumbled across the most obtuse of all Igorots.

Finally the little minx tittered and said: "Father Nobes, why don't you try asking me in English? Perhaps then I shall be able to understand you." Pureza, it seems, had been a pupil in the mission school for several years.

Love of a joke and ease at laughter were characteristic of mission-educated children. It was in startling contrast to the attitude so often encountered in the untutored village people. Perhaps the Christian displayed such a light-hearted spirit in reaction to the oppressive dread under which the pagan Igorot lived. The circumstances in which I first became aware of the great contrast in attitude between the Christian and pagan are still fresh in my memory. I had been calling on our people in the tiny village of Dandanak. As I made my rounds I invited all and sundry to turn up at the Chapel that evening for instruction and prayer.

Seeing one man, perhaps in his 50's, whom I knew to be a pagan, I personalized my invitation as I squatted near him at the door of his house.

"No, Apo Padi, if it were daytime perhaps I would come, but not at night," he said.

"Why not at night?" I asked.

"Because the anitos are abroad at night," he replied, "and something bad might happen to me."

At that moment I saw one of our schoolboys, a lad of about ten, peering out of his timid grandfather's house.

"Pedro," I said to the boy, "you'll be out tonight, won't you?"

"Yes, Apo Padi."

"Then you are not afraid of the anito?"

"Oh, no, Apo Padi," he sang out cheerfully. "Have you not told us that we are under God's protection?"

I am sure that the older Igorot was not a coward, but he had an unhealthy fear of spirits. The man who lives in a world inhabited by so many spirits has to be careful lest he run afoul of one bent on doing him mischief.

That evening young Pedro took the hand of his grandfather and led him through the darkness to the dimly lighted chapel so that he might learn something of the religion which sets men free.

CHAPTER IV

Our biggest problem in developing our mission was not lack of opportunity to go among the people; on the contrary, it was knowing how best to handle the many requests for help which came from so many of the small mountain hamlets.

The first trip I made to investigate one of the appeals to initiate instruction was to the tiny village of Ili-an. The headman had sent word that they would like to have a conference with a priest. It was a gruelling trip. I scrambled 1500 feet down steep slopes, then zig-zagged the same distance up the other side of the canyon, with no trees on either side to offer shade from the blazing sun. Eventually, my interpreter and I reached the plateau on which the small village was perched.

I then learned that I was the first American ever to have visited the village. Still breathless from my climb, I followed the serpentine pathway through the village, skirting plantings of corn, beans, tobacco, camotes and sugar cane, and trying always to avoid stumbling into sunken pigpens which were scattered alongside the narrow paths. Naked little children, their curiosity obviously greater than their fear of this strange white man, trailed along behind us. I finally reached my destination, and, completely exhausted, squatted on the flat paving stones of the central *dapay* of the village. The men, wrapped in cotton blankets and puffing contentedly on rolls of tobacco leaf which protruded from tiny brass pipes, lost no time in beginning the conference for which I had been summoned.

"We want you to come to us often and to teach us about this Apo Jesus whom you Christians worship."

"You know that you will have to give up your own religious practices, with all your sacrifices and feasts?" I asked.

"Yes, we know," replied the spokesman, "but it will be worth it. The Christians we know seem to have rid themselves of something which still plagues us."

"And what is that?"

"Fear," came the startling reply. "They no longer are afraid. They can walk abroad at night without fear. They do not worry about the omens of the flying crows or the running lizards or the creeping snakes. They smile. They are happy, and they live in peace with their neighbors."

"And you people of Ili-an," I asked, "do you still fear your neighbors? I have been told that you are a peaceful people."

"Oh, we want to be peaceful, and it has been several years since we have had any bloody fights, but that is not a condition which will last forever. When some of the people of nearby villages go above our rice terraces and turn the water from our canals into their own, there is always someone who wants to use his head axe. There is too much uncertainty and distrust. The man who hunts today, is himself hunted tomorrow. It is not good. We want to see our people follow the teachings of your God so that there will never again be thoughts of the old ways. Can you teach us?"

On the western horizon, the sun sank behind Tirad Pass. It was this pass which General Aguinaldo's Filipino soldiers had used as they tried to escape from the Americans, after their unsuccessful insurrection at the turn of the century and through which, some 15 years from the time of this conversation, General Yamashita's men would attempt to flee pursuing Americans under General MacArthur.

With that swiftness known only in the tropics, black night rushed in upon us. But we were talking about such grave matters that no one thought of terminating the conference. Someone brought out a bowl of steaming white rice and a smaller bowl of a savory gravy. We patted the sticky rice into little balls and dipped them into the sauce as we continued with our talk.

One of the men spoke for the first time. "My grandson goes to the mission school in Bila," he said.

We all considered this bit of information in silence.

"And you Americans know everything, don't you?"

"Well, hardly everything," I replied as humbly as I could, "but what is it you want to ask?"

"It is a simple question. How high is 'up'?"

It was obvious that the old man was not merely playing with words, or with me, for he was far too earnest. Looking at the expressions on these wrinkled faces as they reflected the dancing glints of the flickering firelight, I could believe that this question had bothered them for some time.

I tried, using as simple terms as I could, to explain that the earth is a ball orbiting the sun, and that "up" is therefore a relative term.

"Ah, then," the old worthy persisted, "you say that the sun is a ball of fire? And is it true, as my little grandson tells me, that the earth was once very hot and is now cooling down—like that ash?" pointing to an ember which had jumped out of the fire.

When I agreed, he continued his questioning. "Then earthquakes are caused by the inside of the earth rearranging itself, just as our fire settles down as it burns?"

It was as simple a way of putting it as I could have devised.

"Then what our ancestors told us is not true? If we are building

39

a house and we feel an earthquake while building, we do not have to tear down our work and begin all over again?"

More questions and answers brought out the fact that it had long been a belief among them that if a person had started a building, and during construction an earth tremor was felt, it was necessary to tear it down to the foundations, offer a sacrifice, and start all over again. Were they to ignore the omen of the quake sent by a spirit, misfortune, they believed, would inevitably befall the builder.

It was not until some time later, thinking over the whole conversation, that I could see the primitive wisdom behind this practice. Undoubtedly during the course of centuries, people had seen some houses collapse inexplicably, while others stood upright. Perhaps someone with an analytical mind had recalled that an earthquake had occurred during the construction of the stricken house. Primitive man, always ready to discern instances of the intervention of the supernatural into his own world, was far more likely to consider the earthquake an omen than to conclude that the tremors might have knocked some supporting posts out of plumb. Many "religious" and "superstitious" practices of people throughout history have just such practical origins.
practical origins.

Whatever the reason for this particular belief, it was obvious that it was regarded as an infernal nuisance by inhabitants of a land where earth tremors occur as frequently as they do in the Philippines.

It was to the great relief of all his listeners that the old speaker at length gave voice to the conclusion he had been reaching for. "If our ancestors were wrong in this, then they may have been wrong in other matters, too. Perhaps, after all, my little grandson knows more than they did. Father, perhaps you had better come here often and teach us old people, too, so that we can be freed from beliefs that have held us to the old customs for so long."

This happened to take place in Ili-an. It might have happened in substantially the same way in almost any other region inhabited by primitive people. Years later I was to hear Kwanyama-speaking Bantu natives of Southwest Africa question the traditional wisdom of their ancestors in much the same way.

The trail of Tadian by way of Bagnen was one on which we took visitors to Sagada who wanted to take a "long hike" deep into Igorot country. One such visitor was a naval captain who had retired from active service and was roaming the world looking for a place to "hang his hat." I was somewhat apprehensive at the prospect of shepherding the "old man" over such a rugged trail, but he had been referred to me by the Bishop, and in those days I was young enough to be a little frightened of bishops.

It was my custom on this long hike across the plateau atop the mountain to stop and stretch out on the forest floor for a few minutes about every half-hour. When I told the Captain that we had reached our first resting place, he said, "I don't need a rest, Padre. I'll just keep going if you don't mind, and after you have rested, perhaps you'll be able to catch up with me." Mindful that this was the forest in which I had once been lost, I would not let him run the same risk, so I kept plodding along. Twice more, as we approached Tadian, I urged him to rest, but each time he insisted on moving along.

At length we emerged from the forest at an altitude of about 1000 feet above Tadian, and looked down at the village with its grass-thatched houses appearing for all the world like a collection of hay stacks drying in the sun. Not pausing even for a moment to admire the view, one of the most spectacular in the entire province, the Captain stumbled along, refusing to sit down for even a moment on one of the many boulders on the steep trail winding down to the village. When we arrived in Tadian in what for me was record time from Bagnen, I was exhausted.

We reached the Chapel and the Captain, without a word, and without waiting for the porters to set up cots, threw himself prone on the floor. In a weak voice he asked me to help him take off his hiking boots. Not until years later, after the Japanese had invaded the Islands and an American signal corpsman, separated from his unit, had hiked into Bontoc after nearly a week on the trail, did I see such bruised feet. Blisters had formed and broken, the skin was chafed off, and I was able to get to his wounds only after soaking off the remnants of his socks.

"Captain, why in the world didn't you take it easy up there?" I asked.

"Padre," he replied between groans, "I was afraid that if I ever stopped walking and sat down, I wouldn't be able to get up."

He told me that he had borrowed the shoes from an army officer in Baguio and that it was the first time he had worn them.

I bathed and cleansed his feet as well s I could with my small first-aid kit. Then I sent a messenger to Sagada with word that we would have to carry the Captain out to the provincial highway the next morning where a car from the Mission should meet us and take us home.

Perhaps it was because he was feeling a little out of sorts due to the mess he had got himself into, or perhaps it was a genuinely frank observation—but whatever inspired it, that evening, as some of our educated Christians sang "Onward, Christian Soldiers," "The Son of God Goes Forth to War" and "Fight the Good Fight with All Thy Might," the Captain muttered to me, "For disciples of Him you call the Prince of Peace, you chaps certainly are a bloodthirsty lot."

CHAPTER V

The Captain had told me that in his quest for a place where he might spend his retirement years, he had been in Formosa often enough to dream that he could be happy there. Unfortunately, a retired naval officer, he said, would not be particularly welcome in a Japanese-controlled area. But he told me enough about Formosa that I felt I would like to visit the Island. So on my first annual vacation I booked passage for Kobe on the *Mexico Maru*, a freighter of the Osada Shosen Kaisha line, with intermediate calls in two ports of Formosa.

I was the only cabin passenger on board, and I received as warm a welcome as visiting royalty might have had when I climbed up the ladder from the launch and stepped onto the deck of the ship. The reason for the cordial welcome became apparent to me at dinner, as we were steaming out of Manila Bay. I sat with the Captain and the ship's other officers, and there was placed before me a printed menu offering a selection of roast beef, roast lamb, roast turkey and baked ham. I was to find a newly printed menu at lunch and dinner each day advertising at least four entrees and a happy variety of vegetables and other side dishes.

The ship's officers had been delighted to see an occidental passenger come aboard. At each meal they politely waited for me to make my choice, and then they had the table steward bring them full western-style meals, after which they topped it all off with various Japanese dishes. The OSK line wanted their first-class passengers to be happy with the cuisine, and naturally the ship's officers couldn't allow good food to go to waste. I'm sure the OSK lost money on my passage.

During the year 1932, the old League of Nations had taken under consideration Japan's aggressive conduct in China, and in the famous Lytton Report had reach conclusions which were displeasing to the Japanese. Just before we reached Kaohsuing (Takao), which was the principal port of entry in Southwest Formosa (Taiwan), the ship's master told me that I would undoubtedly be quizzed closely by the immigration authorities and that I would be well advised to profess complete ignorance of political events.

It was as he had predicted. The number of Americans travelling on small Japanese freighters would not have been great, and the port police were most curious about my reasons for being aboard. They catechized me on the economic conditions of the Philippines, on the political picture there and at home, and eventually got around to their prize question.

"And do you think the Lytton Report did justice to all the facts?" asked my surly-looking inquisitor.

The Captain was standing behind him. He suddenly dropped his cap, which he had been holding under his arm. I was distracted for the moment, which was long enough for me to see him screw up his face in a decidedly negative grimace and shake his head at me.

"Lytton Report?" I repeated. "I am sorry, I never heard of it. I am a missionary, and I teach people about God. I don't know anything about Lytton Reports . . ."

The Captain had retrieved his cap, and he beamed at me as a teacher might at a prize pupil. The official stamped my passport and told me I had permission to travel by train to Taihoku (now Taipeh), the capital of the Island, and to stay there overnight while the ship refueled in the harbor at Kaohsuing (Takao).

The journey by rail was uneventful, and when I reached Taihoku I hurried on foot to the hotel which had been recommended by the Captain. My baggage consisted of a paper sack containing a pair of pajamas, shaving gear, and a tooth brush. I wasn't impressed with the lobby of the hotel, so I asked whether I might see my room before registering, and what I saw I didn't like, so I decided that I would walk around a bit and then go back to Kaohsuing. But I had reckoned without the suspicions of the Japanese Empire.

For perhaps an hour I sauntered around the streets, looking in shop windows, browsing through a little museum—but spending most of my time in the city market. Oriental markets are fascinating. The nose has yet to evolve that can sort out all the delicious smells.

Eventually I found my way back to the railway station and there I checked on the departure of the train for the port city. I found I would have to turn in the ticket which I had purchased and get another. But it wasn't quite that simple. After I had exhibited my passport, with the certificate giving me permission to remain overnight, the clerk in the ticket office became very excited—far too excited to remember much of his English—so within a few minutes a sizeable crowd had collected around the window, and all of the curious onlookers were wondering what trick this strange American was trying to pull.

A policeman soon appeared and escorted me to the station master's office. After a few moments of waiting, a soldier showed up, accompanied by an intepreter.

"You are remaining in Taihoku tonight?"

"No, I shall return to Kaohsuing."

"You told the authorities in Kaohsuing that you would be in

Taihoku tonight."

"Well, yes, I did, but I have changed my mind, and I shall return to my ship."

"Why have you changed your mind?"

What can a person tell proud citizens of a foreign capital? That he doesn't like their hostelries? That the city is grubby and holds no charm for him? That he would rather listen to coal pouring into the bunkers of a ship all night long than toss around on a straw mattress listening to the street noises of a strange city?

"I forgot to bring my camera with me and I can't take any pictures. I have seen all that interests me, so I should like to go back to the ship."

"You told the authorities in Kaohsuing that you would be in Taihoku tonight!"

"Yes, I did, but I have changed my mind, and I shall return to the ship."

"It is too bad that you do not like our city, but the police in Kaohsuing have reported that you would be in Taihoku tonight."

"Yes, and I am sorry to cause trouble, but I have changed my mind, and I shall return to the ship."

"How do we know that you will return to Kaohsuing?"

"Where else would I go? Is there any other place nearby?"

"You may return to Kaohsuing, but you will have an escort."

"I hope he speaks English," I said, "then we can perhaps talk as we ride down. It will be too dark to see the countryside."

I was escorted to the train. By this time, the military had apparently decided that I had no intention of engaging in espionage, for the soldier they assigned to sit near me was a meek-looking youngster, entirely undistinguished in appearance. I didn't even rate a non-commissioned officer.

In Kaohsuing, I found my troubles were not yet over. Trailed by my little military friend, I walked down to the harbor area and looked around for a launch from the *Mexico Maru*. There was none. But I did find a sampan, with its owner sleeping peacefully on its tiny deck. When I said , "*Mexico Maru*," with a rising inflection, he pointed to the ship bobbing at anchor out in the harbor. I scrambled into his boat and took a seat amidship, repeating firmly, "*Mexico Maru!*"

The boatman and my escort engaged in a lengthy discussion, the upshot of which was that the soldier also clambered aboard.

Finally, we pulled away from the dock and glided smoothly away, but not in the direction of the ship.

"*Mexico Maru*," I cried, pointing to it.

"Hai!" said my stalwart sampan operator, continuing on his

course.

"*Mexico Maru!*" This time I really shouted.

"Hai!" he shouted back.

So I relaxed, and within a few minutes we pulled into a dock on the other side of the harbor where a sleepy policeman fended us off while calling for someone to come from the office at the dock's far end.

"You are the American who was in Taihoku and did not like?"

"I am."

"You came here direct from Taihoku without stopping any other place?"

"I did."

"Please to let me see your bundle."

When he had satisfied himself that I had no incriminating documents or other contraband concealed among my toilet articles, my paper sack was returned to me and I was permitted to climb into my sampan without my military escort, and off I went to the ship.

All that the Captain would say about the whole affair was that every country had to guard against spies.

A few days later, the ship docked in Kobe. The Captain had told me I could save considerable money by staying in a western-style Japanese hotel rather than in one usually used by tourists, so I told the taxi driver to take me to the one he had suggested, the "Onsen." We finally stopped before a neat-looking hostelry, clearly identified by a brass name plate as "Minatogawa Hotel." This, I told the taxi driver, would not do. I had asked for the "Onsen," and I was tired, so I stubbornly insisted that to the "Onsen" I would be taken.

He had less English than I had Japanese, so we simply glared at one another until he tried to pull me out of the seat. At that I bellowed for fair, and at length one of the local police pushed his way into the midst of the gathering throng to learn the reason for the row.

It was only after an English-speaking passerby patiently explained to me that "Onsen" was the colloquial name for the formal name "Minatogawa" that I rather sheepishly paid the driver, grunted what I hoped was a dignified apology, and went in to register.

Inside, my language difficulties continued. I found a clean room, but I could not locate the bath. I consulted my Japanese-English phrase book, and found that Japanese apparently say "Furo" when they want a hot bath. Prowling through the corridors until I found a chambermaid, I smiled politely and uttered my little two-syllable word, with a rising inflection. The girl giggled, shook her head negatively, and scampered away.

In my own room I equipped myself with a towel I had found at the washbasin, pushed the room service button, and waited until a young woman shuffled in with many bows. I smiled, and uttered my Japanese word, even adding "dozo" for "please." She, too, looked astonished, giggled a remonstrance, and bowed her way out of the room. I went out into the corridor again and posed my inquiry to several other chambermaids, each of whom had the same reaction as the first two.

Finally, I went down to the lobby to try my luck with the desk clerk, but here, too, I was met with polite bafflement. An interested bystander stepped up to me.

"Please, sir, you are the gentleman who has been making naughty remarks to the girls?"

"Absolutely not," I said, with great indignation. "I am trying to locate the bathroom."

"And what have you said, sir, in so trying?"

"Furo," I said, by now, I thought, rather fluently.

"You mean 'fur-o,' But you have been saying 'fur-yo,' which means, how do you say, a delinquent—a bad girl—one who is promiscuous. You have caused much embarrassment among the girls employed by the hotel, for they are all respectable young ladies."

He carefully explained to me that "Onsen" (he had heard about that episode, too) meant "Hot Spring." This hotel was built over a natural mineral spring, and was famous for its mineral baths.

Soon I was parboiling in a huge tank of steaming water in a common bathroom enjoyed by men and women alike.

When later I reached Kyoto to become the house guest of our Bishop there, I told him of my Kobe experience right away, lest a worse version later reach him.

Bishop Nichols chuckled and said, "Think nothing of it, Clifford. Phrase books aren't clear on pronunciations . . . and as for your bath . . . when I travel into the country, I don't feel I've been accepted by the people until I have had a bath with the ladies of the house."

I took a Dollar Liner from Japan back to the Philippines. Miss Helen Wills, the foremost woman tennis player in the world at the time, was touring the Orient. She travelled one leg of the journey with us and had the misfortune of drawing me as a partner in the deck tennis tournament. We were matched against two of the ship's officers, and despite the handicap of having me as a partner, she very nearly beat the two of them. Whenever I missed the quoit, which was often, she would politely say, "Sorry, partner, I should have had it."

I felt like an oldtimer as we eased our way into Manila Bay between Corregidor and Bataan. As quickly as I could, I left the steaming city of Manila for home and the mountains.

CHAPTER VI

It may sound strange to those familiar with the Igorot only as the head-hunter described in adventure stories, but I can honestly say that I felt more secure among these gentle people than I did among the highly cultured and civilized people of Formosa and Japan. His reputation as a savage was undoubtedly well earned in years gone by, but in the era of which I write, the Igorot was a well behaved, considerate host to strangers who came to live in his land.

In fact, having yielded to civilized disapproval of their ancient custom of decapitating other human beings, the Igorot did not miss, nor often pass up the chance to point out to us the irony of the fact that the most popular picture postcard sold in Bontoc and other tourist centers was one showing a recently severed head resting on the ground and obviously being admired by Igorots sitting around the fire.

It had been the custom to permit a man who had taken a head to tattoo his own face along the jawlines with purple 'X's,' and to achieve a tattooed face was the ambition of many a young man. Many of them were able to satisfy this desire without disapproval during the war years when stragglers fled into the mountains, or when some incautious Nipponese soldier wandered too far from the safety of his barracks.

Anthropologists tell us that the Malayan people have always had an obsession with the human head. Among some of them it is an object of worship. Hence, it has also been considered a desirable trophy. There are still villages in Borneo and New Guinea, inhabited by Malayan people, where the pathways leading into the heart of the village are lined with trophy poles from which heads dangle in various stages of decomposition. Some tribes used to require that an intending bridegroom first produce for his bride's family a number of heads, which would be used to adorn their huts, or to be added to the village's communal collection.

There is much speculation about this fascination with heads. No one among the head-hunters themselves can give a definitive answer as to the reason for it. Perhaps a clue can be found in a practice formerly common in more remote areas of the Mountain Province. There, when an enemy head was brought back by the triumphant warrior, after the traditional dance of victory, a hole would be

47

punched into the skull, using the pick still found on headaxes opposite the chopping edge, and rice beer would be poured into the cavity and stirred up with the brain. The rejoicing victors in the village would then take ceremonial sips of this mixture in the belief that the strength of the slain man would pass into the souls of those imbibing the soul substance of the vanquished enemy. There are other primitive people in widely scattered regions of the world who have believed that the soul is a substance, situated in various parts of the anatomy, chiefly in the fluids and soft tissues.

This belief has given rise to various taboos, such as spitting or depositing one's body wastes in an area where people are buried, lest the dead appropriate the discarded soul substance to the strengthening of his or her own soul and the consequent decrease of the spiritual vigor of the previous owner of the substance.

But primitive man is really not concerned with these explanations. He merely accepts the practice as one of his time-honored customs.

Certainly in a culture in which life was short, the Igorot did not share our horror of violent death. In fact, Lumawig, the tribal man-god, was supposed by most Igorot legends to have come to his people for the primary purpose of teaching them how to make war.

Almost everyone living among a people other than his own succumbs to the temptation to collect souvenirs. I was no exception. I wanted a head-axe. I didn't want one which might have been manufactured the week before by Japanese craftsmen living around Baguio and which could be purchased in countless curio shops of Baguio and Bontoc—I wanted the genuine article—preferably one which had been bloodied. So I let an Igorot friend know that I wanted an axe.

Several days later, one of my favorite converts, a man of about 65, came to my house. He wore a torn shirt over the briefest of loin cloths. His ear lobes, stretched by the insertion over the decades of increasingly larger wooden plugs in holes drilled into them when he had reached manhood, hung almost to his shoulders. When he was comfortably squatting on the floor of my living room, with a serious and fixed gaze into my eyes, he whisked a head-axe from under his shirt and abruptly demanded, "Who is your enemy?"

Startled, I replied, "I have no enemies. What do you mean?"

"You want an axe, don't you? An axe is for killing. So whom do you want to kill?"

Again I protested that I was at peace with all men, and I explained that I wanted only to show this weapon to people in America as an item of cultural and historical interest.

He was unconvinced.

"Now, Padi," he said, dropping his tone to a confidential whisper, "you can trust me. You do not know how to do these

48

things, and we would not want you to get into trouble. Tell me who your enemy is, and I will take care of the matter for you. I know I promised that I would not do such a thing anymore, but for my Apo Padi, just this once, I will. So tell me who it is."

After more urgent and heartfelt assurances that I had no evil designs toward anyone, I managed to convince him that I simply wanted a souvenir.

"But I shall not give my axe to you," he said.

"No of course, I shall pay you well for it, for it is a very old axe. I can see that."

"Nor will I sell it," he countered, "but I will make an exchange. For many years this has hung in my house. In my youth I used it to fight my enemies. I must no longer look upon it with pride. So I shall let you have it, if you will give me a crucifix which I may hang in its place. Perhaps with that before me, I shall sooner be able to forget the wicked things I did before I became a Christian."

The exchange was made, but I didn't feel very good about it.

Although by the early thirties, the Igorot's warlike tendencies had largely been sublimated, we still had to keep in mind that with sufficient provocation there might be a relapse into head-hunting.

Bagnen, nestling on a plateau near the top of a steep mountain, was constantly feuding with Amkileng, situated farther down the slope. The two villages quarrelled endlessly about the rights to the water in the single stream which irrigated the rice paddies of both villages. Especially in the dry season did the argument erupt, for it was then that we had to expect months without rain.

Both places were within my jurisdiction, although the villagers gathered for worship in their own chapels. One day the resident catechist in Amkileng told me that hotheads of both places were beginning to hint that they might settle the recurrent dispute once and for all in the old-fashioned way. After much hiking back and forth and using my youthful diplomatic skills to the utmost, I succeeded in getting the old men of both villages to agree to meet in the Church in Bagnen for a peace parley which I would attempt to moderate.

I studied hard before the meeting. I read all the official decisions on file in the Presidencia regarding this case. These included verdicts reached in Spanish times as well as those rendered more recently.

Most of the legal decisions were in accord. They declared that since there was only one source of water, and paddies belonging to both villages needed the water, amicable arrangements for sharing the flow must be worked out. The latest judgment had even suggested a time schedule for the opening of the various sluices into sectional irrigation canals. I could see nothing wrong with the justice of the decisions, and yet time after time, the men of the two villages would contend that by historic right their people, and they alone, should have all of the precious water.

At the time I was sporting a full beard. It was on our doctor's advice that I had grown it, for I had picked up some sort of skin infection which wouldn't heal as long as I ran a razor blade over it. Certainly it wasn't a thing of beauty, being rather scraggly and a blend of many hair colors, but among a people who by nature had even sparser beards, my prestige seemed to increase in direct ratio to the fullness of my beard.

The morning of the big meeting arrived. When I had greeted the conferees, I asked first one, and then the other opposing spokesman to state the case for his village. Each did so, with no little vehemence. Then, aware of how greatly the Igorot values the opportunity to harangue a crowd, I asked for volunteers to add such information as they thought might be pertinent. When the conference began to drag, after about two hours, I arose and offered my judgment.

It was precisely what had been handed down the last time the matter had been litigated, but I gave it as the judgment of their Apo Padi, who wanted them to live in brotherhood and peace. I added but one proposal of my own. I suggested that each village appoint a number of inspectors who would be charged with the responsibility of seeing that the allotted hours of use of the various canals not be exceeded, and that in no case should an inspection be carried out unless there were an equal number of inspectors from each village.

Then I waited. The atmosphere was tense. Spears, shields and headaxes lay against the walls within easy reach of their owners. Small groups conferred. Messengers flitted from one group to another. The conversation went on and on.

At length the oldest man in the chapel arose. "Here today, my brothers, we have seen wisdom. Apo Padi is a wise man. His years are few, but he has a magnificent beard, and this perhaps shows that he is wiser than his youth might indicate. He has not been among us very long, but he is smarter than all the Spanish *abogados* and American lawyers and Filipino judges whom we have consulted over the many years that we have quarreled about this matter."

"What fairer decision could anyone have made?" he continued. "Of course we must share. And of course we must share in proportion to our needs. Why couldn't the courts have said this? I will tell you why! Because they are not supported by God. But God has spoken through our priest, and what we hear today is His wisdom. We must agree to accept His judgment."

A chorus of approving shouts told me that the day had been won. I never gave the judge whose decision I had merely put into my own words any credit for his work. That would have spoiled it. The Igorot wanted to believe that this judgment was a reflection of God's wisdom through the brilliance of His emissary—me. This was heady stuff for a fledgeling priest, and I had to keep reminding myself that my judgment was hardly original. Still it felt good.

For the Igorots of the first few decades of the twentieth century, before exposure to large numbers of Americans led to disenchantment, we seemed to be the closest thing to a deity which they would ever meet. They knew Americans to be fair, and almost absurdly generous. But they also spotted an inconsistency in the character of the American in their midst. They knew that he professed to deplore the violence which had once been rife in the Igorot country, and yet he never tired of hearing gory stories of the days of old.

There was one ancient native of Bontoc who shrewdly capitalized on this quirk. Over a period of several years he made quite a decent living exploiting the gullibility of American tourists as well as their thirst for bloody stories of the past.

This old worthy, whom I shall call Sagalla, had a deep scarred depression in his forehead, and the remnant of a similar wound on the back of his head. Day after day, he could be found squatting on his heels in the slabstone-paved court outside the low grass-thatched hut which served as dormitory for the unmarried men and widowers of the village. As the tourists gingerly picked their way along the rough stone paths which encircled every hut and crisscrossed the village, he would patiently wait for them to approach near enough for him to go into his act.

He would busy himself with purposeless whittling, and then, when the tourists came within earshot, he would emit a soul-searing groan, drop his knife and his whittling, and press his hands to his head, as if in excruciating pain. This never failed to gain the attention of his prey. As they watched and excitedly babbled among themselves or asked their guide for the cause of the seizure, old Sagalla would gently stroke his head fore and aft, and launch into his tale. The guide would translate slowly, as though hearing the story for the first time.

"When I was a young man," Sagalla would begin, "I was working for a Filipino farmer in the lowlands. It was in the days of the Spaniards—and they were cruel! One day their soldiers came and seized me and told me that because I was a Bontoc they needed me to guide a party of their soldiers into the mountains."

"*Ni, mensakit nan olok!*" (Oh, my head hurts!)

Then after a dramatic pause, while he apparently regained his strength, the story would continue: "Several of us had been gathered together, but none of us wanted to work for the Spaniards. They would promise a peseta, and give us kicks instead." At this point, Sagalla's face would light up with a smile brought on by fond remembrance. "But the Americans—when they came, they would promise a peso and give us two!

"So my companions and I agreed that we would escape from the soldiers whom we were guiding. We made a great try, but just as I had got almost clear of the encampment, a sentry shot me. He gave no warning—he just raised his rifle and shot. The bullet passed right through my head, going in here in front, and coming out here at the back. The pain was great, but I did not faint. I fell to the ground and played dead until the sentry turned his back, and then I ran away. I made my way back to Bontoc by another trail and my father stuffed the hole with carabao dung and hair from the fern tree—that is an old remedy, and a good one—and after many days I became strong again. But some of the dung must have stayed in my head, because it hurts so. Ever since that day I have had headaches. Never since then have I been able to do the work of a man. Now I am good for nothing but minding my grandchildren. It is a sad and cruel thing which those wicked soldiers did to me."

By this time, of course, the tourists had taken the hint and had pressed a few pieces of silver, or even a few crumpled bills into the hand of the old fraud.

Nor did his companions in the dormitory ever give him away, for Sagalla was generous. He always had money for sardines, or corned beef, or some other delicacy with which to enliven the usual evening meal of rice.

One day a tourist who was a doctor asked for permission to examine the wounds a little more closely. His deft fingers probed the depression in front gently, then moved to the back. His hand then went to his own chin and he gravely considered what he had seen and felt. Addressing no one in particular, he said, "Could be, could be, but I wonder . . . "

Actually, Sagalla was the victim of one of the mudfights which used to mark the end of the rice harvest in Bontoc. Many years before, when the strenuous work of harvesting the crop was over, the young men of Bontoc and of Samoki, a village just across the river, would have an exuberant celebration in which they playfully threw mud balls at one another until one side surrendered.

As the mock battle progressed, some of these high-spirited young men packed stones into the mud balls, and one hit with missiles so loaded usually found himself ready to withdraw from the fray. After a number of these affairs had turned into riots, the American Governor of the Province had ordered that such fights, like head-hunting, be stopped. But the decree came one fight too late for Sagalla, who had been gravely wounded, once while facing the men of Samoki, and again a few moments later after he had turned tail and tried to leave the scene of battle.

Sagalla was wise enough to know that American tourists, eager to be titillated by the bloody tales of yesterday, would be more generous in their response to his story of his injury than they would have been had he told the simple truth that he had not ducked at the right time in a friendly mudfight.

CHAPTER VII

It was almost inevitable that we who lived in the tropics where 90 per cent of the native inhabitants were afflicted with one or another kind of intestinal parasite should at some time or other find ourselves similarly stricken. This was especially true of the clergy who had to travel into the outstations where it was almost impossible to take adequate hygienic precautions at meals. Furthermore, we were often expected to partake, in at least token fashion, of hospitality offered so graciously by the people among whom we moved.

Tapuy, a milky rice beer, was certainly one of the world's most exciting drinks—one never knew what he would find at the bottom of his mug. And yet, one could not hurt the feelings of the well-mannered villager by refusing to sip the brew.

In the course of time, I, too, came down with a case of amoebic dysentery. It was after I had had a rather trying time with this disease that Dr. Jenkins told me I would have to go down to St. Luke's Hospital in Manila for an appendectomy.

He told me that he did not want to operate on me in Sagada for several reasons. The first was that the risk of infection for an American in the primitive conditions which prevailed in the dispensary was too great. He said that the Igorots had a much greater tolerance for unsanitary conditions than did we foreigners. The second was that post-operative care would be much more difficult to arrange at Sagada, and would put too great a burden on his over-worked staff.

I was sorry that he felt that way because I knew he was an excellent surgeon. While I was serving as chaplain of the hospital I had seen him perform many times, and would willingly have had him operate on me. Ever since work had begun in Sagada, there had been a dispensary there staffed by an American nurse who was assisted by several Igorots who received their medical training on the job. When Dr. Jenkins arrived on the scene, few native people had any idea of the greater capabilities of a doctor. They thought of him as merely another staff member who would do just about what the nurse had done. After he performed the dispensary's first appendectomy, however, word spread that here was a man who could make one appear to be dead, cut him open, remove the offending substance from the body, and the patient would awaken with no ill effects, never having felt pain during the time he was "like dead." I didn't doubt the doctor's competence at all, but I saw his point that I would be an unnecessary nuisance to the smooth working of the dispensary staff, so I reluctantly agreed with his decision to send me to Manila.

Unexpectedly, an opportunity to travel in a modicum of comfort arose. A private car had come into Sagada and it was due to return over the Mountain Trail to Baguio, whence it would be possible to take a plane to Manila. The only problem was that the barometer was falling rather rapidly.

Until one has experienced a tropical typhoon, or hurricane, one doesn't know the meaning of the term "heavy rain." Baguio, in the southern part of the Mountain Province, lies in such a position that it is battered by almost all of the typhoons which sweep in from the Pacific as well as from the China Sea to cross the Island of Luzon. The word "baguio" in the Ilocano dialect means "storm," and Baguio is well named. To this city belongs the unenviable distinction of having measured in a 24-hour period a rainfall of 44.9 inches.

Baguio itself suffers remarkably little damage in these numerous storms, for the water washes right through the city and cascades down the mountainsides, leaving the residents of the mountain city little the worse for the heavy rains. But the cascading water often brings destruction and death to the lowlands. I was the volunteer "cooperative weather observer" for the Insular government during my years in Sagada, so I had the duty of taking wind, barometric, and rain measurements, and forwarding them to the Central Weather Bureau. The most rain I ever saw in one day was just over 19 inches, considerably short of Baguio's record, but impressive enough to me. In one particularly bad year we had seven typhoons in a period of eight weeks. We did not see the sun for 44 days, during which time some 72 inches of rain fell.

So, when I saw the barometer falling, I knew what might happen. But the doctor told me that he thought I should try to get through to Manila in spite of the threat from the weather. Being young enough to regard it all as another adventure, I set out for Baguio and Manila with a happy heart, a light and feverish head, and an aching groin.

Like the road into the lowlands the Mountain Trail was a single-lane road, guarded by traffic control gates at intervals from ten to 15 kilometers apart.

The storm came up faster than we had anticipated, and before we had made it halfway to Baguio, the heavens opened and the deluge came. Stones and mud kept pelting us as we moved slowly down the trail.

We were traversing a long stretch of straight road, unusual on the Mountain Trail, when the chauffeur and I at the same instant saw a pair of large boulders bouncing down the steep slope at the foot of which our road was built. The driver jammed on the brakes and told me to make a run for it. I needed no persuasion. As the car skidded and swerved, I jumped out and ran, avoiding the mud and rocks as best I could as they came tumbling down. The chauffeur, in the meanwhile, nudged with his front bumper the stones which had come to rest between me and the car, and pushed them sufficiently out of the way to permit him to ease by. The car caught up with me and I jumped back in to ride the last few hundred feet to the traffic gate. Just then a tremendous landslide fell behind us, completely obliterating the road we had just travelled for a distance of about 20 yards.

At the gate a Bontoc-bound bus stood waiting. It had been held until our car should get through. As we passed it we were subjected to a chorus of boos and cat-calls. We later learned that it was three days before that bus was able to continue its journey.

Dr. Jenkins had served briefly at St. Luke's Hospital in Manila prior to coming to Sagada. He knew the staff members there and he had arranged by phone for one of the Filipino surgeons to perform the operation.

As soon as I reached Manila I sought out this surgeon. I was much impressed by his apparent competence as he questioned and examined me. He told me that the operation would be done under a local anesthetic. It was with a mind at ease that I went to bed that night in the hospital.

The next morning I was prepared for surgery and I was fairly groggy by the time I was wheeled into the operating room. To my astonishment I saw there Dr. Beulah Ream, who had a private practice in Manila, and whom I had met socially. I did not see the Filipino surgeon. I assumed that Dr. Ream would be assisting the surgeon who had examined me, but almost immediately it was she who took the scalpel and made the incision. Despite being only semi-conscious, I was able to say, "Beulah, who is doing the surgery?" She replied that she was and that she would explain later.

I remained half-awake throughout the procedure, so I was aware that after she had taken out my appendix she ran her fingers over various other organs in my abdomen. "What's going on?" I inquired.

"Just checking because of your history of dysentery."

She soon sutured the incision and I was wheeled back to my room, where I slept soundly.

When I had recovered enough to be coherent, Dr. Ream came in to see me and told me that the Bishop's wife had thought it not fitting for a Filipino surgeon to be in charge of an operation on an American clergyman, and she had arranged for Dr. Ream to do the appendectomy. This put me in an embarrassing position vis-a-vis the Filipino surgeon, so before my discharge from the recovery room, I asked to see him and I apologized to him for the change of plans. He was most gracious and merely said, "That is all right, Father Nobes. I know Mrs. Mosher, and she has a rather peculiar outlook in certain matters."

A few days after the surgery, Beulah Ream said to me, "You are getting along famously, and all we must be concerned about now is that you do not ·develop adhesions. My prescription for that is activity, so you can begin by taking me to the Army-Navy Club tonight for some dancing. I'll call for you at 7:30."

We spent a pleasant evening at the Club, and along about eleven o'clock my surgeon-date said, "Clifford, as a woman I would like to continue this pleasant evening, but as your physician I think I ought to order you back to the hospital and to bed. Let's go."

My sojourn in the hospital gave me a lot of time to think. I was startled one day when one of the orderlies, an Igorot boy, addressed me as "Apo Jesus." I remonstrated and told him he was being blasphemous.

"Not so," he answered. "You have a beard like Jesus, you are American like Jesus, and you are doing the same sort of work. So I call you 'Jesus.'"

The boy had spent several years in the primary grades in a mission school, and he had picked up an elementary knowledge of Christianity. It was plain to see that it was very elementary for he carried about in his mind a most remarkable collage of Christianity and *Kina-Igorot*, as the native animism was called by the Igorots themselves. He had no difficulty in believing all the legends he had ever heard while sitting in the *dapay* as well as all the New Testament stories about Christ.

The lad was sure that Lumawig, the deity of Igorot legends, had once fed 5000 people with several dried fish and a few balls of cooked rice. Lumawig once raised a child from the dead, and himself had reappeared on earth three days after having died.

It was obvious that at some point in his religious education he had made a transference of the Christ stories to Lumawig, or someone else had made it for him and he had accepted it. I resolved, as I lay there contemplating the implications of this phenomenon, that upon my return to the mountains I would do what I could to arrest the process of synthesis which was apparently taking place.

When I was discharged from the hospital and had completed the rail journey north, our reliable Ilocano chauffer from Tagudin was waiting for me. I told Baldo that I was not feeling very strong, so in his endeavor to get me to bed in the Rest House in record time, we rounded every curve on two wheels. Finally, the inevitable happened. We collided head on with a *calesa* (a horsedrawn two-wheeled carriage) on one of the bends in the road.

What had been a deserted provincial road suddenly became a congested highway, crowded with Filipinos all shrilly blaming Baldo

56

for the accident. We waited in the blazing sun for a policeman to arrive from the nearest station.

The owner of the horse, which had quitely expired, demanded an immediate settlement at a fantastic price for the loss of his animal and for the damage to his calesa. Baldo was willing to give him half of what he asked. I urged that we be permitted to go on to the police station to argue the matter there.

The Chief of Police was inclined to side with the owner of the horse, and as the discussion went on and on, I became more and more faint. Then I had an idea.

I had left the hospital with a large bandage around my waist, so I ripped my shirt out of my trousers to expose the dressing.

"See what you are doing," I said. "The doctor told me I must take a long siesta each day until my wound has healed, and that I might die if I do not get rest. You are killing me. If I die, you will be responsible!"

There ensued a brief and stunned silence. Then the policeman turned angrily upon the owner of the horse and told him that he was a blackguard and a cheat, and might even become a murderer, should I die. Baldo grinned, peeled off a few pesos from his roll of bills, pressed them into the hand of the now-chastened plaintiff, and we were on our way.

CHAPTER VIII

After I had returned to Sagada and was permitted to resume my hikes to the outstations. and to pick up my regular round of teaching in the High School and the Seminary, I began my campaign to clarify the distinction between Christianity and *Kina-Igorot*. I emphasized in class for several weeks the greater reliability of written word over oral tradition. I illustrated from Old Testament stories how tradition could become confused unless constant care were exercised, and I showed how the Hebrews at an early age had schooled themselves in writing so that they might better preserve their oral traditions.

Then, one day, I asked a few of the boys in the High School to accompany me on a hike to Nacagan, one of our smaller outstations south of Sagada.

On the appointed afternoon, our small party set forth, and we headed for the most populous *dapay*, where we found a dozen or more of the oldsters of the village lazing away the hours before the evening meal. It was not hard to get them into a story-telling mood. After they had told me several interesting stories about Lumawig, a few of which had obviously been influenced by Christian legends, I asked them if they would like to hear a story I had heard concerning a peculiar rock formation on the mountainside on the other side of the valley.

As far as I knew, there was no legend about this outcropping of green stone high on the face of the mountain, but I had carefully composed one which I now told. I said that long ago, this had been a rice paddy. It had been constructed by a small boy, I said, whose foster mother treated him so badly that he was hungry most of the time.

Through two seasons the lad had carefully built and cultivated his little rice paddy and at length began to reap a small crop which he secreted in a cave near his village. He used the grain to supplement the meager rations allowed him by his foster mother. The family had noticed the small boy's long absences from the village, and one day his foster mother followed him at a distance and discovered his secret. She appropriated his small store of rice, whipped him severely, and started down to her hut.

Before she reached her home, however, Lumawig suddenly appeared before her, snatched the rice from her and gave it to the

58

boy. With a wave of his hand, he turned the rice paddy into stone, which even to this day, I pointed out, is green like a field of fresh young rice plants. The cringing boy reached out his hand to Lumawig, his protector, and the two of them walked off and vanished. The boy was never to be seen again.

"That story," I concluded triumphantly, "shows how kind Lumawig was to the weak and helpless." I was taking a risk in saying this, for every Igorot who knows his Lumawig knows that this hero-god was a fierce warrior, a tutor of war tricks and tactics, and anything but the gentle Saviour of Christian legend.

But I had carefully planned my strategy, so now I only had to wait for developments.

About a fortnight later, I took the same group of school boys with me, and we went to Data, a village sharing the same mountain as Nacagan, but nearer the top. The two villages had always been friendly, and there was much visiting back and forth.

Again it was late afternoon, and again we found a group of old men who wanted to exchange stories. After a while, one of the men pointed to the outcropping of green rock across the valley and asked me if I had ever heard the story about it. I said I hadn't, and what I had anticipated happened. My "legend" came back to me, altered in a few details, but still recognizable as the one I had introduced into the folklore of the region only two weeks before.

I listened politely and then asked the man where he had heard that story. He shrugged and said that he wasn't sure, but it was probably one his grandfather had told him when he was a little boy.

"And you men," I asked, addressing the others, "have you also heard this story of the rice paddy before?"

"Oh, yes," replied one of the men, "this story is one of our favorites for it tells us how kind Lumawig was to his people."

The significance of my little subterfuge was not lost on my schoolboy companions. They could easily see that there was very little care exercised in passing along folk legends.

One of the greatest strengths of Igorot society, even though it often worked to our hindrance, was the respect the younger people accorded their elders. So I was careful to tell the boys that I did not believe that their old men were conscious deceivers. I said, rather, that their ready acceptance of my story illustrated that because they had such a vast store of folklore, they could not be blamed, illiterate as they were, if they failed to exclude from their treasure of tales one which had been fraudulently introduced.

My contention, I maintained, was proven by the fact that the old men commonly said it was Lumawig who introduced rice culture into a region which formerly had depended upon a diet made up almost entirely of *camotes*. The fact that there had been rice terraces in the Islands long before the tuber had been introduced from South

America by the Spanish conquistadores should have made the percipient Igorot realize that the Lumawig legend could not be true.

My class had learned its lesson well, but I am not so foolish as to think that my experiment had stopped the persistent syncretism between Christianity and *kina*-Igorot. The unlearned Igorot was being thrust into a new world. It was only to be expected that he was somewhat confused and often made errors in his attempts to understand the new and oftimes perplexing culture.

I recall one day running quite accidentally into a great indignation meeting in the tiny village of Payew. The village rice fields had suffered a mysterious blight, and the crop had failed. In casting about for an explanation, one of the elders said it could undoubtedly be blamed upon the great birds which had flown over their fields earlier in the year. It was the first time that the people of this village had seen an airplane.

Now, in their meeting, they were perfectly willing to believe that somehow or other the shadow of the "bird" had contaminated all the fields which it had darkened. They wanted the government to accept responsibility for the loss of their crop.

In those days before the war, life was simple. The natives' attitude towards clothes in the years of which I write illustrates this fact. The Igorot, who in childhood ran naked until he was ten or eleven years of age, could never quite understand the American's feeling about nudity. Out of respect for the foreigners, however, the inhabitants of villages near the automobile roads wore western style clothing more frequently than did their brothers and sisters in the more remote villages.

In areas where the twentieth century had crowded in on them, the Igorot women wore a wrap-around hand-woven cotton skirt, held in place by a highly decorative woven belt, and a short shirtwaist. The men generally wore g-strings, and sometimes shirts or jackets. However, away from the auto roads, the skirts and g-strings were to be found, but few shirts. In the days of planting and harvest, when men and women alike worked in the muddy rice fields, the laborers often sensibly stripped off all their clothes before getting into the mud of the fields. But let an American come into view, and there would be a mad scramble for clothing.

On the trail between Sagada and Bagnen there is a pretty waterfall which serves as a favorite bathing spot of the Igorots from a nearby village. One day as I hurried along on horseback, I made the abrupt turn to the waterfall and surprised a pretty young woman who was taking her bath under the cool cascade.

The bather's skirt was out of reach, and she was too far from any bushes to take cover, so she simply stood on the side of the road, with her hands cupped over her face. Her theory apparently was that it didn't matter what I saw as long as I didn't know who.

On another occasion, when I had completed a long hike to a remote oustation, I hurried down to the stream which flowed by our Chapel, and cooled off with a dip in the refreshing mountain water. A large flat rock formed an island in the middle of the stream, and I crawled up on that to take a sun bath. Moments later, I was startled out of my drowsiness by feminine giggles. I rolled over on my stomach and looked up on the bank whence the tittering had come. Profound silence. I was beginning to think that I had imagined the sounds, when again I heard smothered laughter. This time I could see the telltale movement in the bushes, so I called out in my sternest tones that it was impolite to spy on a person while he was bathing.

"But we mean no harm," came the reply. "We only wondered whether your body was white all over."

Bishop Mosher told me once that while he loved the simplicity of life on the trails, as he made his annual visits to the far scattered stations, he did get annoyed that wherever he went, whatever he did, he could be sure that dozens of big brown eyes would be peering at him.

"When I get sick of it, and really want privacy," he said, "I toss a few coppers in the direction of the shrubs behind which the little scamps are hiding. That gives me a few minutes while they hunt for treasure."

It was not in the matter of clothing alone that we Americans sometimes bewildered the Igorots. Many of our practices were quite baffling to them.

Marriage, for example, was regarded as a good institution, intended to afford a man and a woman a chance to live in congenial companionship and to raise children. But since it is so important that there be children, the Americans were rather short-sighted, the Igorots thought, in insisting that a man and a woman marry each other before they knew whether or not they could produce offspring.

Among the Bontoc people pre-marital intercourse between young marriageables was the usual thing. But this did not mean promiscuous sexual behavior at all. A boy who might crawl into the girls' dormitory at the invitation of one of the girls had better not accept an invitation from another one until it was quite certain that his first mating did not result in a conception. He would be in grave danger of having his hair pulled out and his face clawed if he used this tribal practice as an excuse for casual romance. Marriage was a serious business, and naturally a man had to know whether or not he and his intended spouse could have children before the families would take the trouble to make all the economic arrangements that attended the union of the two families. They couldn't quite see why Americans were willing to take a chance on a childless marriage.

I suppose there were instances of infidelity, but it so happens that in more than ten years of living close to the people, I never heard of a single such case. Divorce was quite rare, too. The usual reason for it was barrenness.

There was a woman in Suyo who had had the misfortune of losing three children by miscarriages. Her husband eventually decided that the marriage was a bad one, and he sent her packing, which apparently caused the poor woman to lose her mind. I was celebrating Holy Communion one day in the village chapel, and in the middle of the service, with my back to the congregation, I heard a loud shriek, *"Asawak! Asawak!"* (My husband! My husband!) I looked back to see this wild-eyed woman running up the center aisle toward the altar. Before she could grab me, however, her father tackled her and carried her screaming from the chapel.

Each time I visited Suyo, I had to expect such a scene. One day, after a long hot ride back to Sagada, I rode my horse up to my front yard, and there unsaddled him and let him roll around before he scampered away to pasture. I had taken my bath and was lying down to rest a while, when in came my houseboy, with the faintest hint of a twinkle in his eye.

"Your wife is here, Father," he said.

I had not realized this woman had followed me, so I was quite perplexed at Jacob's remark.

"Yes, Father," he said in response to my unspoken question, "your wife from Suyo—and she says she is tired and wants me to show her where she is to sleep."

One of the attendants from the hospital came to my rescue on that occasion and escorted my poor little "wife" back to her father's house. Soon after that public sentiment coerced her husband into taking her back into his home. Thus it was that she regained her sanity, and I lost my Igorot wife.

CHAPTER IX

It was never much of a problem for me to decide where or how I would spend my annual vacations. When one is closed in all year long by high mountains, he wants nothing more than to be able to stretch his vision, unimpeded by hills, to distant horizons. So, whenever possible, I elected to spend my holidays near or on the sea. Inter-island travel in the Philippines before the war was somewhat of an adventure, unless one used the well equipped, spanking new S. S. *Mayon*. That vessel was for tourists and "softies." Most residents of the Philippines preferred the other ships, tubs which seemed to be held together with chewing gum, piano wire, and faith. A round trip to Jolo, in the Sulu archipelago, on one of these relics then, was not only a delightful excursion through some of the most glorious sea lanes in the world, but held the added element of pleasure from the thrill of meeting the unexpected.

For me, the unexpected started happening the moment I walked into the steamship office and asked for a first-class round-trip ticket. The clerk was astonished.

"First class!" he said incredulously. "Don't be foolish, Padre, buy deck passage. You'll sleep on deck anyway—it is too hot in the cabins—and if you want some privacy for dressing, you can always give the cabin boy a few pesos and he'll make a cabin available for you."

My next surprise occurred after I had been on board the ship a few hours. A young American woman had been looking at me rather intently. Evidently she decided that my clerical collar rendered me harmless, for she came over and introduced herself, and then startled me by saying, "Won't you put your cot alongside mine tonight?"

I must have looked embarrassed, for she blushed in turn and protested: "Oh, I know that sounds bad. What I mean is, I don't like that dark-skinned man over there. He has started flirting already and has told me that he intends to set his cot next to mine tonight. I shall be next to the rail, the steward arranged that, and I should like to know that my neighbor inboard isn't going to make any passes at me." It was a compliment of sorts, I suppose, so I made the necessary arrangements with the deck steward.

During the next few days, as we stopped at Cebu, Iloilo, and Zamboanga, my deck mate, whose name was Margaret, and I found

63

ourselves chumming with each other and with a man named Mr. German, who was a substantial businessman in Jolo. He kept promising us that if we thought the stops in the intermediate islands were interesting, we would indeed be enthralled with Jolo, which was at the extreme southern tip of the Philippine chain of islands, and he promised to show us around.

We had a little more time in the turn-around port than in ports along the route, and Mr. German was as good as his word. He took us ashore to his luxurious home where we had lunch. Then his chauffeur drove the three of us into the back country for a good view of the bizarre scenery that makes Jolo unique. While driving along, he suddenly said, "By the way, would you like to meet the Sultan of Sulu and his harem?"

What visions flitted through Margaret's mind I don't know but in my imagination I was immediately transported to Bhagdad. I had mental pictures of dusky beauties slithering over polished floors in titillating dances.

Would we ever!

"His Highness is Jamalul Kiram II," Mr. German said. "The great sorrow of his life is that he has no son to succeed him—nor even a daughter. The apparent successor to the throne is his niece and adopted daughter, Princess Hadji Piandao, whom they call the *Dayang Dayang*."

Mr. German went on to tell us that when the United States took over the Philippines from Spain, a special treaty with the Sultan of Sulu was negotiated by which the Sultan's spiritual authority over all the Mohammedans of the Philippines was recognized. He was also acknowledged to be the legitimate owner of scores of tiny islands, most of which virtually disappeared at high tide, lying between Sulu and North Borneo.

The British, too, we were told, admitted the Sultan's authority in North Borneo, and in acknowledgment of his contribution toward the pacification of the fierce sea-going Dyaks and other Mohammedan people of those areas, the Crown paid him an annual pension.

Mr. German told us further that the freak typhoon which had blown through Jolo in 1932, the year before, killing over 200 people, and devastating the coconut groves and mangosteen plantings, had also made a shambles of the Sultan's palace. I hastily revised my imagined picture of dancing girls in lavish halls, but still retained a notion of an extensive and luxurious palace, made the more interesting by wreckage left by the storm. It was about then that we passed through an opening in a barbed wire fence, and found ourselves in a large yard in front of a typical Filipino hut standing on bamboo stilts, with a thatched roof, and off in the back a detached cooking shed, roofed with thatching and galvanized iron.

"Why are we stopping here?" asked Margaret.

"This is the palace," grinned Mr. German.

A formidable looking Moro, with an ornate bolo hanging at his waist and a revolver tucked into his belt, came over to challenge us.

Mr. German said a few words in the local dialect, and the servant smiled and retreated to the house.

But he was back quickly and said, in English, "The Sultan is having supper. He cannot see you now."

Mr. German was almost apoplectic in his anger. "What do you mean, he can't see us now? You go back and tell the old man that I, Otto German, am waiting, with two guests, and if he doesn't come out to see us right now, he can ask somebody else to lend him money in the future."

How much the messenger understood, I don't know, but apparently it was enough. He fairly flew back to the "palace" and then we saw him dart out of the back door and into the kitchen cookshed. Then out from the shed came the Sultan, His Highness Jamalul Kiram II, Sultan of Sulu. He had a rice bowl in one hand, and a china spoon in the other. In his haste to stay in Mr. German's good graces, he had not even bothered to put down his meal. He was a slender, elderly little fellow, with a rather soiled white linen suit, of the old-fashioned kind that had a stand-up collar, which today we call "Nehru jackets." He wore a red headband, as was the custom of the Moros, and he was bare-footed. Trailing along behind him came several rather slovenly Moro women.

"Hi, Apo German," he said, "welcome to my poor house. And welcome to your guests. And my wives give you greeting, too." Then, in a lower, more confidential tone, he lapsed into the local dialect in which language Mr. German replied.

Then, turning to us, Mr. German explained: "He is worried about my threat not to lend him money. He hopes to build a better house as soon as he can beg, borrow, or steal enough money to buy the supplies. The new 'palace' won't be much more elaborate than this one, but he invites us all to return when it is finished."

"You have a good time with Mr. German?" asked the Sultan of us. "He is a good kind man."

After a few more pleasantries were exchanged, we made our farewells and rode back to Jolo, still, despite some disenchantment, impressed that we had been in the presence of and had conversed with a reigning monarch.

CHAPTER X

Even in the routine of everyday living among the Igorots, there was always the possibility of excitement.

We had 50 boys from a dozen different villages, some of which had been deadly enemies for centuries, inhabiting the same dormitory, rubbing elbows in the same mess hall, and tilling the soil in the same garden patches. They were like boys everywhere—volatile, aggressive, and high-spirited. In bringing these lads into such close contact, we were generally successful in encouraging lasting friendships between those whose forebears, given the opportunity, would have enthusiastically decapitated one another.

But in taking this calculated risk, we had also created an explosive situation in which even a slight misunderstanding could erupt into a major catastrophe.

We had to watch school-boy quarrels closely, lest a boy from outside Sagada carry back to his home village tales of persecution or mistreatment by schoolmates of erstwhile enemy villages. Hotheads at home, who harbored misgivings anyway about allowing their youngsters to sojourn in enemy territory even for such an important purpose as getting an education, might easily destroy the delicate truce which existed between the villages.

This dormant hostility was not peculiar to the schoolboys. We had to be careful in assigning teachers to outstation schools, so as not to make the error of placing a *maestro* in a village against which his own people had warred. To do so would mean that the maestro would most likely be fearful of exercising discipline in the classroom lest he be charged with partiality. Nor could teachers from actively feuding villages be asked to work together.

Out of necessity, we once placed teachers who had come from traditionally hostile villages together in a remote outstation school. At first, they seemed to get along well, but as the term wore on, and they began to feel the strain of teaching, they became more and more impatient with one another.

Eventually a bitter quarrel erupted. One of the men was shot through the leg.

It was his allegation that the other teacher had pulled a gun and shot at him, and that only his quickness in striking down the other man's arm had saved his life. The accused denied that he had ever had his hands on the pistol, or that he had even seen it.

Each teacher had his own set of partisans who, as they accompanied the principals into Sagada to seek medical assistance for the wounded man and to bring the matter to the attention of the Mission authorities, loudly argued the cause of their own champion.

It was significant that the men by-passed the Presidencia and the town authorities and came directly to the mission hospital and asked to see the clergy.

While the injured man was being treated, we were questioning the witnesses. The protagonists of the patient firmly repeated their charges that their man was the innocent victim, and those of the accused as loudly maintained that their friend was blameless.

Not knowing how we could possibly reach the truth of the matter, we were seriously considering calling for a formal police investigation, when one of the hospital attendants whispered that we would do well to examine the wounded man's trousers. However, they were not to be found. No one on the hospital staff could remember having put them anywhere, and they certainly were not hanging around Pedro's waist.

The pressure was mounting. The teachers had come from hostile villages. Already the report of the shooting was on the way back to the homes of the men involved, and soon delegations from each village would be starting for the Mission, intent on seeing that their own native son come out on top in this quarrel.

While asking Pedro to go over a couple of points in his version of the incident, I noticed, almost casually, that he had a much bulkier pillow than the standard hospital issue. When the likely reason for this occurred to me, I snatched the pillow from beneath his head and pulled from the pillow case the missing trousers.

It was no wonder the lad had tried to hide the garment. One leg was bloodstained, as was to be expected, but there was no bullet hole through the cloth. Instead, the pocket had been ripped out, and there was a distinct scorch mark on the inside of the pants leg. Pedro had obviously been shot by a pistol while it was still in his pocket, and it seemed a fair inference that the wound was self-inflicted. The attendant had noticed the severe powder burns around the leg, and had surmised the rest.

Confronted with the evidence, Pedro had to admit that he had shot himself while struggling with the other teacher. He insisted, however, that he had tossed his revolver over a cliff as soon as the quarrel had been interrupted by those who had come running at the sound of the shot. We were never able to find the gun.

His colleague was so relieved at being exonerated that he was perfectly willing to drop the whole matter. Both he and Pedro agreed to tell the elders of their respective villages that it had been a senseless quarrel, and that they were once again friends.

Episodes similar to this one arose frequently enough to keep us in the Mission from growing bored. We never really knew from one day to the next whether we were going to be called upon to argue the superiority of Western medicine over sacrifice to the *anito* for the treatment of pneumonia, or whether we were going to have to dissuade some aggrieved schoolboy from going home in anger further to inflame smouldering hatreds between ancient enemies.

Just as the *anito* were blamed for all misfortunes, so also many happenings quite unrelated to tribal enmities were twisted around by partisans to demonstrate that ill will still existed.

In those days we kept a small stable of horses on the Mission compound to carry us to the various outstations. As they ambled over the grounds, grazing as they wished, they would often shatter the quiet of the day by getting into fights. In one of these battles my stallion received a bad kick which knocked out his eye, and we had to destroy him.

As some of the Mission employees dug a burial pit we sprinkled the carcass liberally with quicklime. The next morning there was a gaping hole where there had been a horse grave the night before.

The doctor was notified that he would probably soon have a procession of patients complaining of collywobbles, but to our amazement, no one turned up at the infirmary seeking help for any ailment which could be attributed to eating quick-limed horse meat. It was not until weeks later, while I was visiting in one of the outstations, that I learned the reason for this.

"Those Sagada people whom you employ in the Mission are most unkind," said a man in the Tanulong congregation to me.

"Why do you say this?" I asked.

"They tried to kill us by putting poison on that horse which they buried," he replied. "They knew we were watching them bury the animal, and they knew that we would dig up the good meat and take it back to Tanulong."

"But none of you were sick, were you?" I asked.

"No," he said, "because we saw their scheme, and we washed off the poison before we cooked the meat. But you must admit, they tried to kill us."

I might as logically have accused a gatekeeper on the highway of trying to kill me several weeks later when I was shopping for a new horse to replace the one that had been eaten.

I had heard that an Igorot in the village of Utokan had a spirited young horse for sale. I made an appointment to inspect him. He had already been saddled when I arrived, and his owner was holding the bridle tightly as I mounted. The moment I was in the saddle, the horse took off down the road like a three-year-old at Churchill Downs on Derby Day. He would not respond to the reins, but galloped at will, truly a runaway. Ahead of me I could see that the barrier gate was down, and my horse was racing right for it. I knew very well that no Igorot horse was a jumper, and the barrier stretched across the road at just about the height of my chest, so I had quick visions of my impending death as I shouted out in pure fright, "Open the gate! Open! Open!"

Just as I reached the gate, it flew up, and I passed under it safely. The horse finally ran himself out and I was able to pull him around and return to the prospective seller.

"He is fast enough," I said, breathlessly.

"Yes and you ride well, too, Apo Padi, especially on a horse which has never been under a saddle before," came the matter-of-fact rejoinder.

CHAPTER XI

The daily routine at Sagada was never dull. Every day started at the altar, either in the main church, at 6:30, or if it was a day when I was to visit an outstation, the farrier would bring my saddled horse shortly after daybreak in order to insure that I would reach the chapel in time to conduct a service before the people had to go into the fields or the forest for their daily work. The day the Padi visited the outstation was the day of worship for the people of that village, although a good many of them living within five miles of Sagada would hike into the central station on Sunday.

My primary responsibility was to prepare candidates for ordination, so even on days when I had an early morning service in one of the outstations, I would conduct classes upon my return to the central station. I usually taught from 8:30 until noon, and again from 3:00 p.m. to 6:00 p.m.

I tried to take one day off each week to do as I liked, reading to prepare my lectures and sermons, for example, or relaxing by exploring the caves south of Sagada. Those caves never ceased to fascinate me. The entrances were few and usually well hidden by thick shrubbery. Just inside the cave entrance one would inevitably find crude coffins, made by hollowing out massive trees. The coffins were most often empty, and skeletons were scattered around them, grim reminders of the way pagan Igorots disposed of their dead, and of how dogs had no respect for them.

The corpse was stuffed into one of these undersize coffins, with the legs bent so as to bring the knees up to the chin of the deceased. With the body there was usually placed a bit of rice and such of the person's cherished possessions as he might need on his journey to the afterworld – typically a walking stick, or a favorite tool. All too often, though efforts were made to place the coffins on high ledges inside the cave entrances, dogs would find them and succeed in tipping them over. Sometimes the natural process of dessication and decay would unbalance the containers and cause them to topple from their precarious perches.

A man of substance was treated rather differently. His body would be placed in a hardwood chair, under which a slow smouldering fire would be ignited. The corpse was thus gradually dried out. This would take about as long as it took the mourners and other friends to impoverish the family of the deceased by feasting on his cattle and other animals and emptying his granary. Then the corpse, nearly mummified by this time, was stuffed into a full length coffin and lodged on a ledge in one of the caves.

So a walk, or more accurately, a crawl through these caves was an interesting, if gruesome, experience. Add to the hazard of crawling over bones and upturned coffins the constant threat of encountering bats or other rodents, and it was not an experience for the fastidious or faint-hearted. Behind the house in which I lived during my second term of service was a so-called "bottomless pit" into which our drain pipes emptied, as well as being the place where whatever trash and garbage we generated was dumped. That it was not indeed bottomless I discovered one day while crawling deep into a nearby cave to investigate the source of a beam of light which had intrigued me. It took me quite some time to clean myself up after that crawl.

All deceased people were not buried in caves. For instance, a woman who had died in childbirth would be buried by the pagans in the ground with needles stuck into her open palms. This was to make it too painful for her to flap her hands and arms at night and thus, in jealousy, fly around and bring harm to babies who had been safely brought into the world.

It was widely believed by the non-Christian Igorot that if a woman was delivered of twin babies, it was the duty of the father to take one of the twins out into the forest and abandon it there. The theory was that twin births were unnatural, that one of the children must have been born because the woman had been impregnated by a spirit, and that it was necessary to give the spirit one child lest he take both of them.

One of my students told me that he was a twin, and that he was apparently the weaker of the two babies at the time of birth, so his father put him out to die. But the next day the child who had been spared developed pneumonia and quickly died. The father then rushed back into the forest and rescued the abandoned one. Twenty-five years later, on a return visit to the Philippines, I particularly wanted to see the mother of this former student. The man was now a priest. His mother had gone blind, but when, without having been told that I was in her village, she heard me call her by name, she immediately recognized my voice and cried out, "Ho, that is my 'Apo Padi!' "

Blindness was not uncommon among the older people, and when one saw how smokey their homes were, with the smouldering cook fire burning most of the day and night and no way for the smoke to leave the hut except through the thickly thatched roof or the lungs of the residents of the huts, one wondered why all the people living in such conditions did not develop eye trouble. Many of them also suffered pulmonary weakness and disease because of their constant

71

inhalation of smoke.

An Igorot village in the early morning or in late afternoon looked like a field of smouldering haystacks, as smoke seeped through grass roofs. Edward Longid, my interpreter and companion through so many months of my life among these people, once remarked to me as we approached Sagada and saw among the smoking huts a few new roofs of galvanized iron, "More beauty for Sagada!"

I replied, "Yes, those thatched huts are lovely to look at."

"No, Padi," he said, "I mean the iron roofs."

"But, Edward," I said, "you surely can't think that a metal roof is a thing of beauty."

"Oh yes, Apo Padi, I do mean that; you have never lived in a grass-thatched hut. The insects live in the roof, and rats go after the insects, and then snakes crawl in for the rats. A metal roof is clean. So when I see one, I am happy for the village, and think, 'More beauty for Sagada.' "

In addition to the class work and rounds of visits to outstations, life was often enlivened by the excitement of native feasts, or *cañaos*. Before planting, or before harvest, or after the passing of widespread illness, or for any of a number of other reasons, the village elders would decide that it was time to have a cañao. This meant that the people could lay aside their daily tasks and devote themselves to feasting, dancing and singing for several days.

It was then that many of the people would discard their Western clothes and the men would don their woven g-strings, and the women their woven skirts and abbreviated blouses.

Their dancing was accompanied by the rhythmic beat of the brass *ganzas*. During a cañao, as the villagers concentrated all their efforts on merriment, the Christian converts would often ask whether they, too, could participate. We always responded that as long as they did not take part in the offering of sacrifice and prayers to the anito, they could in good conscience enjoy the fun.

The arrival of the Bishop for an official visit, during which he would confirm hundreds of candidates, was always an event to be looked forward to. The Igorots, pagan as well as Christian, would flank the road leading to the Mission and, dancing wildly at the head of the procession, lead the car carrying the Bishop to the Church. It was a time of joy not only because his presence meant that many of them would at last be given full communicant status in the Church, but also because it would be the opportunity for them to send messages back to Manila to the Governor General about any grievances they might have.

Bishop Mosher was an excellent companion on the treks to the distant outstations. He would ride a pony or hike, as the trail permitted, along with us, and he was perfectly willing to put up with the inconvenience of camping out for the few days that the visit to the outstations required.

I recall one trip especially well. We had ridden and hiked to Kate-ngan, about six hours from Sagada. Upon arrival I had set up our cots in the school building, taking the usual precaution of placing the legs of the folding cots into metal pans of kerosene to thwart any bedbugs that might have had designs on our tender flesh. However, the weather was particularly sultry, so the Bishop asked whether we might set up the cots outdoors in the playground area instead. I did so, taking the additional precaution of rigging a mosquito net over the cots. I then set them alongside one another in order to make the one large net serve both cots.

In the middle of the night, I heard the Bishop muttering and then his hand came slapping down on my face as he shouted, "Damn you!" Naturally I was awakened and alarmed. "What did I do, sir?" I asked. "Not you, Clifford, sorry to disturb you. I didn't mind it as long as that mouse or rat stayed down at my feet, but I didn't like it when he crawled over my chest and face. And now we'll have to pull the net apart to see if he's still hiding someplace in the blankets." We did, and he wasn't, so we rearranged our cots for what we hoped would be the rest of the night.

But as the night wore on, I became aware of a curious snuffling sound coming ever closer to our cots. I lay tense and anxious, and finally I caught the distinct odor of a water buffalo which was intent on investigating the invasion of his usual nocturnal resting place by these strange creatures. I flashed on my light and this so startled the animal that he stumbled into our cots, overturning mine and dumping me onto the ground.

"Don't you wish you had a nice civilized diocese someplace in the States?" I asked the Bishop as we set up our cots for the third time. "Nope. Too dull there. If you can survive it, this is the life."

Carabao (water buffalo) are reputed to dislike the smell of white men. One foggy morning on the way to Suyo, a station near Sagada, I dismounted and led my horse through a sunken path, afraid that he might stumble on a rock in the fog, which was so thick that while I held the reins in one hand, I felt my way along with the other. Suddenly I touched more than damp air. It was the south end of a carabao.

He and several of his companions had apparently spent the night in the sheltered ditch through which the path led. He snorted violently, but the ditch was too narrow to permit him to turn around to see who was tickling his rear end, so instead he butted the animal in front of him, who, in turn, pushed his neighbor ahead of him, so within a minute the entire group was in panic trying to get out of the ditch. My horse, in the meanwhile, was unhappy at the turn of events and was tugging furiously on the reins trying to get back to the safety of his stable. I managed to quiet him and pull him through the now vacated ditch and resume my journey to Suyo.

Suyo was the first outstation I had ever visited. That visit had taken place in 1931, while I was still a deacon. It happened just before Christmas Day. Father Rose had given me a sack of peanuts and sent me there to have a prayer service, and to promise the congregation that he would be down to administer the Sacrament of Penance and to give them their Christmas Communion as soon as he could. He told me that I was to give the peanuts to the children after the service. I was instructed to get up into the belfry and tell the children to gather around below. Then when they were in place, I was to scatter the peanuts among them.

"They'll love it," he said. "They always expect peanuts at Christmas time." He also gave me a few pieces of paper-wrapped taffy to toss to the youngsters.

In obedience to his instructions, I threw peanuts and candy down to the happy throng of children below. They scrambled eagerly and hilariously for the treats.

These were the same youngsters who would later be offering themselves for training as teachers, catechists, priests and nurses.

So along with peanuts and taffy, we were sowing the seed of life in Christ among them. From that throng of children in Suyo I know of at least three who are now ordained clergymen teaching children who are as they themselves once were, babes in the Faith but growing into stalwart Christians.

CHAPTER XII

Our years in the Philippines were enriched by our friendship with one of the most remarkable men I have ever known.

I first met Dr. Hilary Pit-a-pit Clapp soon after I reached the Philippines for work in Sagada. It was on All Saints' Day, 1 November 1932. The magnificent new church, named All Saints, had been built for the Bontoc Mission and it was to be consecrated on this day. Igorots from Bontoc and the dozens of villages all around had crowded into the edifice for the celebration. The service concluded, they were now sitting around, gossiping, visiting, waiting for the cooks to announce that the carabaos, cows, and pigs were sufficiently cooked for the feast to begin.

An incredibly old man was squatting on the ground near the portico, hacking away at his toe nails with a wicked looking bolo knife, the blade of which was at least a foot long. I turned to a Bontoc who had been pointed out to me—a short, stocky, well-groomed man dressed in an immaculate white linen suit, and I said, "Dr. Clapp, you had better stick around. It looks to me as though that old fellow might miss and chop off one of his toes."

Dr. Clapp smiled and said, "Oh, no, my father can take care of his pedicure quite nicely. He'll be all right."

It was typical of Dr. Clapp that he never tried to hide his humble origins. He was born in a thatched hut in the village of Bontoc. He was schooled abroad under the patronage of the clergy of the Mission. He had dined in the homes of the socially elite on Park Avenue, but he was never ashamed of his father, a man who wore a g-string in preference to trousers, and who in general appearance differed not a whit from any of his contemporaries in Bontoc. Dr. Clapp was a truly selfless and brilliant man. Pretense was alien to him, until, during the war years, he played a role contrary to his nature, and as a consequence, lost his life.

Pit-a-pit was so named at birth for a type of bird that lives in the rice fields. He was said to be handsome as a youngster, strong, lithe, and bright. While Pit-a-pit was still a pre-adolescent, there came to Bontoc in 1903 a priest of the Episcopal Church, the Rev. Walter C. Clapp. Father Clapp's instructions from Bishop Charles H. Brent had been simple and straightforward. He was to establish a permanent mission among the wild head-hunting Bontoc Igorots. Missionaries of other Christian groups had from time to time made the attempt, but thus far their efforts have been in vain. Father Clapp knew he was faced with a difficult task, but he seemed to know, too, that in doing God's work, one must be patient, so he set about learning the dialect and carrying on his routine priestly life.

Soon he became aware of the fact that he was being watched daily through the window of his house by a good-looking little Igorot boy. Not wanting to frighten the lad, he waited for him to make the first advance. Pit-a-pit was as curious as any little boy would be. When he could no longer restrain himself, he asked Father Clapp the meaning of all he had been witnessing.

Father Clapp told him, little by little, the story of Jesus, and of the desire of the Heavenly Father that all people, wherever their homes, whatever their race, call upon His name. The boy was entranced. Soon he asked whether he, too, could be baptized and become a brother of Jesus.

Pit-a-pit became Hilary, an appropriate name for one who was always loved for his ready wit and flashing smile. Hilary was a leader among the other youngsters of his age group and he soon had organized a class of candidates for baptism. Day by day he helped Father Clapp with his language lessons, and in turn, he began learning English. Father Clapp conducted a primary school of sorts in which Hilary and some of his companions were introduced to books.

Hilary was not content with the primary education the poor school at Bontoc could offer, so he went, despite the misgivings of his parents and many of his tribesmen, into the enemy country of Benguet, to enrol at the Episcopal Church's Easter School in Baguio.

Even this was not enough for the ambitious lad. He was now fired with the desire to use his active mind in the service of the God he had grown to love. He knew, however, that he would need further education. Father Clapp gave Hilary his own family name, and with the help of Bishop Brent, sent the eager young boy to Trinity College School at Port Hope in Ontario, Canada.

Hilary Clapp returned in due time to the Philippines, now persuaded that he could best serve his people as a medical doctor. He enrolled in the University of the Philippines and eventually was graduated from the medical school, being the first of his tribe to advance so far into the twentieth century.

In the meanwhile, the pioneer work of Father Clapp had been growing apace. The government, too, had been widening its services to the people in the Mountain Province. Consequently, there had been established a small dispensary. The Bontoc Igorots were beginning to learn that all illness does not come from the machinations of the evil spirits. Dr. Clapp, determined to use his talents among his own people, volunteered for the Government Health Service in the Mountain Province and in due time was stationed in

Bontoc. The Governor General recognized his ability as a leader among his people and appointed him Representative in the Legislative Assembly for the Mountain Province. From time to time he was offered promotions in the health service. These would have carried him into better paying positions in the more "advanced" provinces but far away from his beloved Bontocs. His answer was always the same—God had made him a Bontoc Igorot, God had provided for his training, so, in gratitude, he would serve God by serving his fellow tribesmen.

Stories of his courage and leadership are many. Two will suffice to show why the people trusted and loved him.

There was the time when Dr. Jenkins, the American missionary doctor in Sagada, urgently invited him to assist at a difficult operation.

A woman with a terribly swollen and bruised abdomen had been brought into the dispensary. The witch doctor of her village had diagnosed the case as "infestation by a crocodile." Despite the severe beating her family had administered in an effort to kill the animal in her belly, no crocodile had emerged.

Dr. Jenkins knew that if he operated and lost his patient, his practice, scarcely begun, would probably come to a halt then and there. Yet delicate surgery was necessary to remove the ovarian cyst which he suspected to be the cause of the swelling, and he needed Dr. Clapp's assistance in performing it.

The invitation put Dr. Clapp into a difficult position. Bontoc and Sagada were enemy villages from centuries back. Should he assist and the patient die, he, a Bontoc, might be charged with having killed a Sagada woman. On the other hand, should he refuse to help, the Sagada villagers might make the accusation that he, a Bontoc, would not lift a hand to help a suffering enemy.

Despite these circumstances, neither doctor hesitated. They operated, and they made the old witch doctor watch the whole performance so that he would see for himself there was no crocodile inhabiting the patient's insides. The woman recovered. Pictures of her holding a jar containing the cyst were taken and sent throughout the area. As a result, the surgical practice of Dr. Jenkins' ministry was greatly advanced.

The other incident which showed Dr. Clapp's courage as well as his place in the affection of his people occurred after I had become priest-in-charge of the Bontoc Mission in 1940.

The fact that Raymundo, our cook, had spent hours honing the blade of his bolo to razor sharpness was not in itself alarming. Nor was my inability to locate Philip, our houseboy, noteworthy. Ordinarily it would not be significant that our few Tukukan boys were missing from their usual haunts. The boys' dormitory at All Saints Mission was set in the midst of a larger compound. The boys might be anywhere.

But all of these facts taken together were enough to cause me some concern. Raymundo, a native of Sagada, had been talking wildly that morning about "these crazy Bontocs" who were determined to kill every Igorot from enemy villages in reprisal for the rumored murder of one of their own boys by some men from Tukukan.

Philip was a Tukukan and before he had come to us, I had had to pledge to his parents and village elders that he and every other Tukukan boy whom we accepted in our dormitory in Bontoc would be under constant guard and would be quite safe in our Christian compound. The trail between Bontoc and Tukukan had been trod for centuries by fanatical warriors from one or the other village intent upon hunting heads.

The villagers were usually very close-mouthed about matters like head-hunting. They knew that Americans took a peculiar view of this centuries-old practice of theirs. However, feeling was running high and enough incautious remarks had been made to worry me a great deal.

The headless body of a young adolescent had been found on the trail leading to Tukukan. A Bontoc boy was missing. Two Tukukan men had been seen skulking around the outskirts of the village the day before. The men of Bontoc put these facts together and came up with the conclusion that murder had been committed by Tukukans against a Bontoc.

I had gone through the village that morning to see for myself what might be brewing. Never before had I seen so many of the Bontoc elders gathered in the meeting places in front of their dormitories. They all seemed to be fussing over little fires on which they were cooking chickens which had been killed as sacrifices to the ancestor spirits. Ancient hardware in the form of spears, headaxes and bolos, which had for years hung on the walls of their huts, had been taken out and had been honed and polished. Wooden shields rested against the stone walls of the tiny yards of the dormitories. I could hear the chilling cadences of the war chant emanating from far corners of the village. At the usual loafing places on the sun-drenched main street of the town, the younger men of the village quickly looked away as I passed, as though sharing some guilty secret which they didn't want their priest to discover.

I had been through several similar experiences in my years among these primitive mountain people, and each time the hotheads had been talked down by the more cautious. But it was different today. There was a sense of determination which had been lacking before. Preparations had gone much further. There were no giggling girls watching their young men strut about. Any question about the intention of the village to carry out its retaliatory raid vanished as an angry mob formed and moved down the street which led through the Mission compound. This was the river road to Tukukan, the one which had been travelled by warriors of both villages many times in the past.

As the mob came closer, I rushed into the rectory and called out, "Philip! Philip, where are you?"

"Here, Father, in your room," came the muffled response.

When I entered the room, I had to search before I could find him. Quaking with fright, too terror-stricken even to reply to my questions, he was huddled inside a laundry hamper in the corner of the closet. Tightly grasped in his hand was a meat cleaver which his friend, Raymundo, had whetted to a keen edge. I told him to stay just where he was until I returned.

I then hurried out the back of the house and over to the boys' dormitory. With the help of some of their Bontoc schoolmates, all the Tukukan boys were well hidden in the storage room, with empty rice sacks, vegetable baskets, or spare blankets thrown over them. Each had a bolo or similar weapon close at hand.

By this time the mob was so close that I could distinguish individual voices.

I knew that the Filipino lieutenant in charge of the local Constabulary detachment had left town hurriedly at noon. As rumors of trouble had spread, he had "found it necessary" to carry out an inspection in Payew, ten kilometers from Bontoc in the opposite direction from Tukukan. The Governor, too, was out of town.

However, even had they been in Bontoc, I still would have turned to Dr. Clapp, for I knew that he was the only man who would be able to control the frenzied head-hunters. I hurried to his house at the edge of our compound.

As I raced across the compound, I recalled the occasion when he had had to stand up to the assembled witchdoctors and frightened warriors of a small village in the hinterland where smallpox was raging. With his vaccination kit he was there to help them, and they, in their superstition, were convinced that the only thing that could help them was sacrifice and prayer to the anito. They had no desire to have the meddling Western-trained doctor tell them how to behave, and they told him so. But he had stood his ground, had vaccinated everyone he could catch, and the epidemic had stopped.

"God grant that he can stop these men," I prayed. Juanita, his wife, saw me coming. "The doctor is not here," she called out. "I have sent up to the hospital for him. You had better delay the mob if you can."

Back to the other side of the compound I flew, just in time to intercept the leaders of the gang as they were storming into the compound heading toward the boys' dormitory.

"No, you don't!" I called out. "You stay right where you are."

"Father, we mean no harm to you," said one of the men, "but there are some Tukukans here, and we want them."

"There are no Tukukans here," I lied. "Don't you think I have enough sense to know what you have been planning? I sent them home last night."

At this the leaders of the mob hesitated, and much talk flew back and forth. My frantic groping for my next words came to an end as I saw Dr. Clapp hurrying towards us.

"Men of Bontoc!" he shouted as soon as he had scrambled up on a stone wall and could see the whole crowd. "What madness is this? Do you not love your home, your wives, your children? Would you go off to Tukukan to kill and thus cause the Americans to send in soldiers who will arrest you all and send you to the lowlands where you will rot in jail? Ah, you stupid men! I am ashamed on this day that I am a Bontoc."

"Perhaps you have forgotten that you are a Bontoc!" one leader shouted derisively.

"Yes, he has forgotten!"

"Yes, truth has been spoken—he is more like an American!"

"He forgets the bravery of his fathers!"

I was worried, for I had never before seen such disrespect for Dr. Clapp. But the insults might never have been shouted for all he seemed to care.

"Fools of Bontoc—I will not call you men any longer, for men would stop to think this matter through—you are fools who rush for your axes first and think later. Fools of Bontoc, hear me!"

The angry murmurs subsided.

"You think you are going to avenge the honor of our village. You will do it by killing any man, woman or child of Tukukan whom you can find, even if the child is sucking the breast of its mother! Yes, indeed you are brave men! And why do you do this? Because you say one of our Bontoc children was killed yesterday. But give me a few minutes and I will show you what complete fools you are."

As he spoke he seemed to be looking for someone to come from the main part of the town.

"Ah, here is the *maestro*. I will let him speak to you," the doctor shouted as he helped the teacher, a lowlander from Ilocos Sur Province, to the top of the wall.

"Maestro," Dr. Clapp said, "where have you just been?"

"I have just come from the constabulary headquarters," he replied.

"And what did you see there?"

"I saw the body of a young boy."

"Do you know whose body it was?"

"Yes," replied the maestro, as a startled silence settled over the group, "he was Manuel, my houseboy, the son of my cousin."

"He lies!" One of the men in the crowd shouted.

"The boy who was killed is Fan-oy, of the Chilas neighborhood."

"Oh, you stupid fools," said the now enraged doctor. "Fan-oy is in my examination room at the hospital. He went there last night. I didn't know it was he you thought was killed. Have any of you seen the body in the constabulary barracks? It is the body of a lowlander. The skin is evenly colored, not lighter around the loins like that of Bontoc boys who wear g-strings instead of pants. The soles of the feet are not tough like yours—because Manuel wore sneakers most of his life. And for this poor lowland boy you were ready to go to Tukukan with murder in your hearts. I know of no Tukukans who would be brave enough to kill a Bontoc right on the edge of Bontoc village! I wonder which one of you killed Manuel. But I will not ask. All I want you to do now is to go back to the village and put away your weapons. And next time, don't endanger our whole village, when you don't even know whom you are seeking to avenge.

The crowd melted away, asking no more questions, demanding vengeance no longer, for each man suspected strongly that the murder had, indeed, been committed by a Bontoc rather than by a Tukukan, who would have been brave, indeed, to have invaded Bontoc territory to commit such an act.

Had it not been for Dr. Clapp, ugly things would have happened that day. The people knew it, and respected Dr. Clapp for what he had done.

In the years to come even greater demands would be made on Dr. Clapp's diplomacy. Eventually, his selflessness and devotion to God and his people would result in martyrdom.

CHAPTER XIII

Despite frisky unbroken horses, landslides, disease and tribal feuding, I had not only lived through the six years of my first term, but I had enjoyed almost every day of it. In the spring of 1937, the Bishop gave me permission to go on regular furlough to the States.

Being just about half-way around the globe, we had the option of travelling west through Asia and Europe, or east across the Pacific. I opted for the western route, and accordingly, I booked passage on a British freight line, which normally called at numerous ports in the Dutch East Indies, Malaya, and Ceylon and proceeded through the Suez Canal into the Mediterranean before crossing the Atlantic to the United States. But it was 1937, and Benito Mussolini had embarked on his great adventure in Ethiopia, so the Suez Canal and the Mediterranean were closed to commercial traffic. From Colombo, therefore, the ship had to take the long way around the Cape of Good Hope, 30 days out of sight of land, to Dakar in French Equatorial Africa before striking out across the Atlantic to Halifax and then to Boston and New York.

Due to an unexpected change in sailing schedules, I had only two hours in which to pack all my things and get out of Sagada on my way to Manila. That was probably history's quickest and sloppiest packing job. My houseboy and I simply laid the trunks open on the floor and jammed clothes in wherever they would fit. When I reached Boston, the customs officials asked me to open one of the trunks. I warned them. We opened one anyway, and everything popped out. A kind officer helped me squeeze it all back in and didn't bother with the rest of my luggage.

That trunk remained unopened from that day until I returned to the Philippines exactly one year after I had left on furlough. When my houseboy opened it, he looked a bit puzzled and said, "But this is just as it was when we packed it. Did you not change your clothes the whole time you were away?"

Fortunately, it happened that we had thrown all my tropical clothing into that trunk, so I had no need for any of it in the States. I had to warn my mother against opening it, and I know she often was sorely tempted to do just that. I remembered too well the heroic struggle of the customs man to shut the trunk in Boston, and I had no desire to go through that again.

The trip home had its adventures. While the ship made numerous coastal calls between Surabeia and Batavia (now Djakarta), a small group of us had hired a chauffeur and car and had driven overland the length of Java. We then went on to Singapore, in which port the ship's company hired most of its Malayan crew, and where we sweltered in the harbor for a full week.

It was just after leaving Singapore that I was suddenly stricken ill. I blacked out, and when I came to I found that I was afflicted with a grand case of diplopia. Although I had no symptoms other than double-vision, the captain decided that he would have to put into the nearest Sumatran port and leave me in a hospital. We had no doctor aboard, and he was responsible, he said, for my welfare. He certainly had no desire to have on his ship someone who might fall down a ladder and break his neck. I could see his point, but by appealing to his patriotism I successfully overcame his caution and persuaded him to take me on to a British-staffed hospital in Penang instead of to a Dutch one in Sumatra.

I was in that hospital in Penang for several weeks until I regained the normal use of my eyes. None of the doctors were able to explain what had happened except that I had suffered some sort of hemorrhage behind one eye. (It was not until months later that a doctor in New York determined that I had had a slight case of Burger's disease, a malfunction of the circulatory system due to excessive smoking.)

Penang and, in fact, the whole British Commonwealth, was in a gala mood during these weeks. George VI had been crowned and celebrations were taking place all over the world. As long as I was to be delayed, I was thankful that the interruption took place when it did, for there were concerts, special athletic events, and all sorts of extraordinary celebrations on the social calendar.

Finally, after a month of hospitalization and recuperation in a boarding house inhabited by young British businessmen, I was able to continue my trip on another British ship.

Travellers in Oriental countries often wonder whether the ubiquitous Chinese shopkeepers would not cheat their own mothers to turn a profit. I can testify that there was at least one, in a precious gem shop in Colombo, who had some humane feelings.

I had picked out a lovely set of amethyst jewelry, and I was engaged in the usual process of bargaining. My highest offer and his lowest selling price were still many rupees apart, but my long stay in Penang had been expensive, and I had literally figured down to the dollar how much I needed to get home and how much I could spare for this purchase.

I resolutely stuck to my highest offer, and assured the proprietor of the shop that the price I had named would take all the money I had. He seemed disinclined to believe this, so I emptied my pockets onto his counter. He looked over my passport and tickets for the remainder of my voyage, carefully counted out the money, and picking it up, he shoved the set of jewelry over to me. Then as I turned to leave, he said, "But it is very hot. You are far from the ship." Handing me back a few rupees he said, "Here, hire a rick-shaw boy for the trip back to your ship."

* * *

In that I was able to renew friendships and have time with my family, the furlough was a joyful period of my life. However, it was not a time of rest. The Bishop had told me that upon my return to the Philippines he would release me from teaching in the Seminary which had been established only if I recruited other priests who would continue the work. I had become much more interested in evangelical work in the outstations than in teaching in the Seminary, and I had asked for a change of assignment.

I travelled far and wide telling the story of the ministry in the Philippines, thanking congregations that had helped support the work by sending "special" gifts, and making new contacts that might later be beneficial to the mission. Always I was on the lookout for young priests who might respond to my invitation that they consider working in the Seminary we had established. As a result I was able to recruit five young priests, all of whom subsequently received appointments by the National Council and turned up for work in various capacities in the next few years.

The National Council had a strict rule that a missionary on furlough should not handle money gifts which might be made to his work. I thought this shortsighted because I had found that people are far more willing to give to projects than to budgets, especially if they are moved by a personal plea after the work has been described. It was in this way that the magnificent plant at Sagada had been built. But the logic of the Council was that a spellbinder might move people to contribute to his project while equally important work might languish for lack of support because the men and women who were doing it did not have the chance to travel about to explain what they were doing.

In theory, the Council rule was a good one, but in practice many a dollar could have been raised if missionaries on furlough had been encouraged to urge people to give "specials" to a particular project.

I had found as I travelled about that people would say, after hearing a description of the work, "And how can I help?" I wanted permission to take a gift here and there, so one day I asked Dr. Lewis B. Franklin, the treasurer of the National Council, what I should do in the event some individual or congregation proferred a gift for the work. "Take it, and give them a receipt, but don't tell Dr. Wood I said this."

Dr. Wood was the Executive Secretary of the Board of Missions. I asked him the same question a little later. "By all means take whatever is offered whenever it is offered, and give them your personal receipt. But don't tell Dr. Franklin about it."

So I left personal receipts all over the United States and sent the money back to the Mission in Sagada. Such gifts made it possible for us to do work which was not anticipated when budgets were drawn up. It also permitted us to offer scholarships to boys and girls who otherwise would never have been able to go to school.

The busy furlough days drew to a close and shortly before, leaving home on the return journey to the Philippines, I received a note from a woman I did not know. She introduced herself in the letter as a refugee teacher from the China Mission. The Japanese Army had moved up the Yangtze Valley and as a result she and the other staff members carrying on the Church's work in Yangchow had been compelled to flee. She had been evacuated to Manila, and was working temporarily at the Chinese school operated by St. Stephen's Mission in Manila.

She further wrote that she had been forced to leave almost all her possessions in Yangchow, but that another teacher had managed to pack one suitcase with some of her things and had sent that to the Mission office in Shanghai. She asked me if I would pick it up in Shanghai and take it on to Manila where, she assured me, she would meet my ship at the pier and take the suitcase through customs.

My agreeing to this simple request changed the whole course of my life.

Florence Moore had always, from the time she was a schoolgirl in Philadelphia, hoped that some day she might become a missionary in China. All through her college days at Temple University she maintained this objective. She prepared herself for her chosen career by taking, in addition to her courses in Education at Temple, courses in Religious Education at the Church Training and Deaconess School, which was also in Philadelphia.

One day a visiting missionary on furlough from China spoke at the University and said that there was an opening for a teacher at St. Faith's School for Girls in Yangchow. Florence volunteered at once.

So now, after several years, the girl who had dreamed of teaching in China found herself a refugee from that country temporarily teaching in a Chinese school in Manila. Officially, she was still attached to the China Mission and on loan to the Philippine Missionary District.

When my ship reached Pier Seven in Manila, I was hanging over the rail searching the crowd on the dock for the young woman whose suitcase I had retrieved in Shanghai. I saw a lovely young lady who was just as anxiously searching for some one on the deck. She saw me in my clerical collar and tentatively waved. I waved back and the thought crossed my mind that if that was the girl from Yangchow, I was going to initiate a campaign to make her my wife.

She was and I did. However, it was not until the third day that I worked up enough courage to ask her to marry me.

The next two weeks were pure delight. We saw each other as often as possible, which meant morning, noon, and night. Members of the Mission stationed in Manila wanted to know why I didn't leave town to return to my station in the hills. One of the women who had also been evacuated from the China Mission guessed what was going on and cabled Bishop Roberts of Shanghai that if he didn't recall Florence Moore to Shanghai, he would probably lose her to the Philippine Mission.

So Bishop Roberts cabled Florence that he had a job for her to do in Shanghai and that she must return at once.

With the cable clutched in her hand, Florence went to see Bishop Mosher and told him that the developments of the past fortnight had made her change her plans. She now wanted to take her regular furlough and go home to think about those developments before making any decisions.

The Bishop recognized at once that he was about to acquire one of the finest workers who had ever reached the Orient, so he cabled Bishop Roberts in Shanghai that he had had his chance and had muffed it and that Florence Moore was returning to the States on regular furlough.

She did, to return six months later to become my bride.

I suppose that Florence would have been a little frightened had she foreseen the happenings in the Philippines in 1941-45—that she would be behind enemy lines during an invasion, that she would be expected to feed a sick husband and two sick children when there was no food to be had, and that she would be told by the doctor that her children and her husband would probably not survive their imprisonment by the Japanese.

But I rather think, from the way in which she met every crisis during those horrible years, that she would have smiled and said, "We can make it, as long as we don't get too excited about it all, because, after all, we aren't alone."

While I can clearly recall practically every day of my first term of service, strangely I find it more difficult to bring into sharp focus things that happened in my second term. Perhaps this is because I had assumed another role, that of husband and father, and the novelty of life among people of a different culture had worn off to some extent so the impressions are not as clearly etched in memory.

Of course there are exceptions to this general vagueness. Who would forget his wedding day?

We were married at seven o'clock in the morning. It was early enough to avoid the sticky heat of Manila's midday (and early enough for the noon edition of Manila's daily paper to carry the story of the wedding).

We went to a quiet hotel at Pagsanjan Falls for our honeymoon trip and tried to act like an old married couple. We thought we were getting away with it, when the table boy in the dining room laid the paper carrying the photograph of us before the altar down in front of us saying coyly, "These people look like you, do they not?"

Every visitor to Pagsanjan Falls shoots the rapids below the cataract. Skilled boatmen carry one passenger at a time in the frail-looking bancas, and in the quick trip through the white water, it seems that the little craft ship as much water as is left in the river outside. Ours were no exceptions. As our separate bancas cascaded in single file through foam and past deadly looking rocks, I was wondering how my widow would carry on without me. Just then, I heard her cheery laughter, and decided that it couldn't be as bad as it seemed to me. I got a thorough soaking, but I survived unscathed. Florence told me that she had been laughing because she found it ludicrous that while I was sitting waist deep in water in the banca, I used my hand not to steady myself, but to hold aloft my camera. Such priorities amused her, but, then, she was not a photographer.

From Pagsanjan we went to Corregidor to spend a few days with an artillery officer and his family. Little did we dream that in a short time this grim fortress rising out of Manila Bay would be reduced to rubble, and that its entire garrison would be killed or captured.

We also accepted an invitation from the Admiral commanding the 17th Naval District to spend a few days at his Commandancia at Cavite. That building, too, was soon to be totally destroyed in a bombing attack.

CHAPTER XIV

Thoughts of war were far from us when we reached Sagada after our wedding trip, ready to abandon my bachelor apartment and move into a large house which was available. We fully expected to spend the rest of our missionary career in Sagada. We liked it there. It enjoys the sort of climate that God must have made to retire to. Its five-thousand-foot altitude, and its location in the tropics, mean it has no extremes of temperature which ranges from 50 to 85 degrees, and the beauty of the landscape cannot be excelled.

Green hills rise from the broad valley. Generations of men searching for firewood had almost completely denuded the mountains, but the Igorot had learned that without an arbor his springs were apt to dry up. Hence he trims off branches for his firewood, and leaves the almost perpendicular trunk standing nearly naked with only enough branches growing at the very top to let the tree survive.

Cozily hugging the contours of the hills are groupings of rice terraces. They are yellow, silver, green, or brown, depending upon the degree of maturity of the plant. On hillsides which cannot be reached by life-giving streams, there are more terraces, dry, and in varying shades of green depending upon whether the plants under cultivation are beans, camotes, corn, sugar, or tobacco.

Only occasionally is the quiet of this secluded mountain town disturbed by the raucous noise of traffic. One is far more likely to be kept awake by the song of the crickets.

We liked the people. We liked the reason for our life among them. We liked being a part of a self-sufficient little group, linked together by a common and worthwhile purpose. We were content.

The Sagada compound was almost extra-territorial in its independence from the Province and the country around it. We had our own well-stocked general store. We grew our own vegetables on our own farm. All of our buildings were interlinked by a privately built and operated telephone line. We had a hospital which was adequate for most medical needs. Even our water supply came from our own mountain spring.

The water was piped into all the Mission buildings, and there were in addition a few hydrants set around in the village adjacent to the compound, so that the people there might have access to the spring water. Despite the fact that we believed that our water supply was safe, we nevertheless took the precaution of boiling it before consuming it.

One day our doctor told us that he was treating a lot of gastro-enteritis. There had been no cañao during which spoiled meat might have been eaten. Nor, at first, did the doctor suspect the water supply, for nearly all of those who were ill were residents of that section of town which was supplied by the Mission's supposedly pure water supply.

However, since close investigation showed that each case was directly traceable to the hydrants in the village, we had to assume that the water was contaminated. That no people living on the Mission compound were affected could be explained by the fact that we didn't drink our water raw.

The doctor and I trudged into the hills, carefully inspecting our water main for any signs of breaks as we traced it to the source. When we reached the spring whence the supply came, we found our trouble. Over the course of time, through the storms of many years, the fence posts set around the spring area had rotted and the barbed wire barricade had fallen to the ground. The spring bubbled up out of the marsh, and a herd of water buffalo had found the area precisely to their liking. The huge beasts were blissfully wallowing in our drinking water.

We fetched from the spring several vials of water and sent them to the Provincial Department of Health for analysis. Why everyone who had been drinking the water raw hadn't died we'll never know. The report from the Health Department looked like a catalogue of all known intestinal diseases.

The upshot of it was that we had to construct a slow sand filter through which we might pass the water before it reached our kitchen faucets. Because of the variety of contaminants in the water, a slow sand filter was all that could be used. Chlorination took care of the bacilli of bacillary dysentery, but we had also to contend with amoebic dysentery, and the chlorine could not penetrate the surrounding shell of the encysted amoeba. They had to be filtered out through the sand. Other micro-organisms which we had learned were in the water were taken care of either by the chlorine or by the sand in the filter.

It cost much money which I raised by telling the story to well-wishers whom I had met on furlough. We had a great deal of trouble maintaining the filter, which, at the time we constructed it, was the only one in the Philippine Islands. However, the peace of mind and freedom from disease which resulted was worth the expenditure and the trouble.

Our dreams of a quiet ministry to our little enclave of Christianity in a region of paganism were soon interrupted when the priest in Baguio went on a year's leave and the Bishop called upon me to take his place. Although Baguio was the metropolis of the mountains, its mission staff was much smaller than that in Sagada. The work was different, too. For the most part, it was a chaplaincy among Igorot students at the Trinidad Agricultural High School and among Igorot laborers from the north who were under contract to the various gold mines which surrounded the city.

Then, as now, Baguio attracted many retired folk who appreciated the salubrious climate. There was, for instance, the doctor's widow who was terribly fond of dogs. It preyed on her mind that, contrary to municipal ordinances, out in the Trinidad Valley there could generally be found a lively trade in dogs among itinerant Igorots in from the villages. These mutts were the most miserable looking specimens of canine life that could possibly be imagined—flea-bitten, skinny to the point of emaciation, and battered by ill-treatment from their human masters as well as from fighting with one another.

These dogs were sold for table-meat. Igorots would purchase them for a few coppers and fatten them up before feasting on them.

This appalled our gracious American widow, and as she moved about among the peddlers she alternately scolded and purchased. There were times when she had as many as a dozen dogs in her home. Whenever she went out to dinner, she took several of them with her. Always she would try to find good homes for the animals she had rescued. Should she fail in this endeavor, they could still be assured of a comfortable living with her. Her human visitors might have to wait patiently for a seat to be vacated by a just awakened dog when they visited her, and they might leave the house surreptitiously scratching new flea-bites, but there were few of us who did not sympathize with Mrs. Saleeby's campaign to keep man's best friend off the Igorot's dinner menu.

Baguio was a much smaller city then than it is now, but it was still a good cross-section of American civilization, and it was comfortable there if one didn't mind an annual rainfall of approximately 200 inches, mostly compressed into a four-month period.

We knew that we were not to live there permanently, so we never really let our roots sink too deeply. Nevertheless, it was a pleasant year. While we lived in Baguio, our first child, Penelope Anne, was born.

Still, it was with much joy that we welcomed the regular priest back to his station, for we had been expecting that upon his return we would be ordered back to Sagada.

This was not to be. The priest in charge of All Saints Mission in Bontoc, the capital town deep in the heart of the Mountain Province, had left permanently for the States, and the Bishop asked me to take charge of that station.

A London cockney transplanted to the gullah region of South Carolina would have an easier time conversing in his new home than I had in using my Igorot dialect in Bontoc. The two languages were grammatically akin, and much of the vocabulary was identical—if it appeared on paper. When spoken, the differences were enormous. For the several years that I was in Bontoc, I was labelled as the priest who spoke with a Sagada accent and vocabulary.

I was to find that for two reasons the Bontocs were less amenable to the preaching of the Christian Gospel than were the people around Sagada. First, they were so much closer to the main tourist routes, being right on the provincial highway, that they had many contacts with Americans who were not dedicated to the conversion of souls to the love of God. This made them more indifferent to Christianity than their brothers in the more remote areas who knew only Americans who were there to help them. Secondly, from untold centuries past, the Bontocs were a much fiercer and more warlike people than those of any other tribe of Igorots. Enmities between villages were more lasting, grudges were more dangerous, and the preaching of a gospel of brotherhood was more alien to their nature.

This animosity between natives of different villages caused us to keep closer watch on the lads in our dormitories than had been necessary in Sagada. Boys from regions which had been at odds with each other had to be kept apart for the first year of their residence in the Mission compound. By the end of a year hereditary hostility had usually vanished.

One of our dependent villages was Balili, where the dialect and customs were more similar to Sagada's than to Bontoc's. At the other end of the territory in which we ministered, a distance of perhaps 20 miles, was the tiny village of Ma-inet. In the old days Ma-inet had produced some of the most ferocious warriors of the mountains. Balili, however, had always been considered a peace-loving village.

One day the dormitory master came rushing into my home to tell me that a Balili boy had stabbed one from Ma-inet. The Balili had apparently been tormented and persecuted in petty ways until he had reached the limit of his endurance, at which time he had whipped out his knife and slashed the shoulder of his chief oppressor.

After tending the injured boy's wounds, I hustled all over the compound, looking not only for the offender but also for two other boys from Balili. My intention was to give them refuge in the Rectory, for I knew that as soon as word of the trouble spread, vengeance would be demanded. But as quick as I had been to institute the search, the boys I was seeking had been quicker. They had grabbed their few precious possessions and were running back to Balili as fast as their legs would carry them.

I phoned Sagada to tell the clergy there of the trouble we had had, for affairs like this had many ramifications. In some mysterious fashion word had already reached Sagada, 15 miles away, and the Balili boys up there had likewise fled to the safety of their own village.

My next move was to hasten to Ma-inet, a beautiful but gruelling hike from Bontoc. The path was laid out in Igorot style, straight up the mountain with practically no zigs or zags. The tiny hamlets of Ma-inet and Guina-ang, which lay close to one another in this secluded corner of the Mountain Province, are seen by few outsiders, which is a shame, since in my opinion, there are no lovelier vistas any place in the Islands than those to be seen on that climb.

The mountains are steep and only lightly wooded. The hills fold into deep ravines the walls of which are step-laddered with rice terraces all the way from the floors of the valley nearly to the peaks. Intricately placed canals carry water from one ravine to another. Terraces in Banaue and in other parts of the Province may be more stupendous, but I know of no place but Ma-inet and Guina-ang where one can look down at tier upon tier through branches of pine trees which dot the steeply ascending trail. Because of the crumpled face of the mountains, the terraces are narrow and high, unlike the broad fields clinging to the hillsides in Banaue, and the overall impression is that only rugged determination to wrest a living from an inhospitable environment could have produced the rice paddies which fill the terraces. The effort in building and mud-packing to make fields leak-proof which must have gone into the construction of a paddy that does not measure more than 20 square feet of arable land is unbelievable.

The village of Ma-inet is unique in that in its center is a large hot spring which bubbles out of the ground. The name "Ma-inet" actually means "boiling water." The stream which originates at the spring winds through the village and its route can be traced from any place in the village by the clouds of steam rising from its surface.

My purpose in climbing the trail to Ma-inet was to assure the family of the victim and the village elders that the wound was only superficial, and that the whole episode was merely the result of the thoughtless quarrel of two quick-tempered boys.

There were muttered threats and some of the men wanted to go on the warpath at once, but wiser counsel prevailed, and the village leaders agreed to await the recovery of the wounded youngster and hear his story before taking any reprisal.

It was at times like this that we felt we were sitting on the edge of a live volcano. And yet, once they had become better acquainted, boys from traditionally hostile villages would as often as not share the same cotton blankets on chilly evenings.

Residents of the Mountain Province try their best to remain off the highways in the month of July. It is then that typhoons sweep in from the China Sea, often bringing massive mud slides and closing the road for days at a time. However, our second child was due to be born early in July 1941, so, learning from the weather bureau that

92

there were no typhoons headed toward us we hired a car and were driven down to Baguio, where we stayed with the Rev. Sidney Waddington, who was priest-in-charge of the Mission of the Resurrection.

On July 7, Jane Elizabeth put in her appearance at the Hospital Notre Dame de Lourdes, where Penny had been born 22 months earlier. As soon as it was safe to travel we returned to Bontoc. Among the congratulatory notes was one from High Commissioner and Mrs. Sayre, whom we had met socially while in Manila some months before.

In October the Sayres came to Bontoc on an inspection trip and had tea with us at the Rectory. I took advantage of their visit to talk to the High Commissioner about my upcoming furlough. I told him that I had already booked passage for the whole family to sail in January 1942, but that I was somewhat apprehensive about the prospects of war in the Far East and that, if he thought it safer, I would arrange for Florence and the little girls to leave earlier and for me to follow in January. He said he didn't think that it would be necessary, for while he was almost certain that Japan and America would eventually go to war, that would not happen until February at the earliest. He felt that we would be safe if we departed as planned.

It was not until 1945, when we finally reached home, and I was summoned to Washington to testify at a Senate hearing, that I learned that the government policy back in 1941 had been to discourage the exodus of American civilians from the Islands, lest the Filipino populace draw the conclusion that America was preparing to abandon the Philippines. As one of the senators observed, "Actually you people were pawns and suffered through the war as a result of a considered government policy."

This hearing, incidentally, contributed to the decision to compensate those who had remained in the Islands throughout the war from premiums collected by the War Damage Corporation.

We were all invited to submit a claim to cover the loss of our household goods and other property. But the settlement amounted to far less. From the limited funds available, priority was given to those business firms which had suffered losses, and which intended to renew their activities in the Islands. In this way the economy of the Philippines could be reconstructed. Then compensation to educational, religious, and medical facilities was made. Various other categories of businesses and institutions were aided.

When all of these demands were satisfied, the claims of private individuals were considered. In the end my family's claims were adjusted downwards until we received only about ten percent of our monetary loss. However, most of us agreed that to rebuild the economy of the newly independent Philippine Republic was a far more urgent requirement than to compensate private individuals.

CHAPTER XV

December 8 (December 7 on the eastern side of the International Date Line) was eagerly looked forward to because it was the Feast of the Conception of the Blessed Virgin Mary, the day on which the Mission of St. Mary the Virgin in Sagada observed its patronal festival in those early days.

Florence and I, along with both little girls, who were scheduled for a medical check-up in the Mission hospital, were in Sagada on this day in 1941. So were hundreds of other people from out of town, there to participate in the day-long celebrations. I had escorted our baseball team from All Saints Mission, Bontoc, up to Sagada. My Bontoc boys and the Sagada boys were playing for the championship.

I don't remember what the score was, but Bontoc was ahead, for the first time in several years. Suddenly one of the missionaries came dashing down to the field to tell us that the radio station in Manila had reported that the Japanese had attacked Pearl Harbor. Our reaction was "so what?", we had a game to finish, and "where was Pearl Harbor, anyway?" Furthermore, continued this kill-joy, Japanese planes had been reported over Baguio, and that was only 100 miles away. "Well," we figured, "we still might have time to finish the game." And, he went on, unconfirmed reports were that all reservists were being called up and that all trucks and cars were being commandeered by the military to transport them to the shores of the Gulf of Lingayan, where Japanese landings might be expected.

Well, we certainly didn't want to be stuck in Sagada for the four or five weeks that it would take to dispose of the Japanese, but, we argued, since Sagada was host, and Sagada was behind, Sagada ought to forfeit, which they did. So I corralled my boys, told them that they had won, loaded them into the trucks, picked up my wife and the little girls at the hospital, and hurried down the hill to Bontoc.

Excitement was running high in the provincial capital. Panicky residents were making a run on the various food shops, stocking up on whatever canned goods and staples were still available. The few of us in town who had cars were scurrying about buying five-gallon tins of gasoline, and then looking for safe and inaccessible places in which to hide them (ours went into the belfry tower of the church).

Young men were running about with such military gear as they

94

had. In some cases this consisted only of a military sun helmet. Because of a parsimonious congress and the early concentration of America's war preparation efforts in the European theater, our reservists had trained with wooden guns. It was not until they reached the beaches of the China Sea with orders to repel the Japanese landings, that many of these lads at last held real rifles in their hands.

But on that day in Bontoc a holiday mood prevailed. This was the great adventure, and the inexperienced young soldiers were jubilant as they scrambled into the trucks waiting to take them to the south. Most of them would never again see their beloved mountains. Ninety percent of the Philippine Army was killed or imprisoned within a few months.

It seemed silly to us that our good friends, Yamane, Yoshikawa, Sato, and others should be arrested by the Constabulary and thrown into a hastily organized concentration camp. Certainly they were Japanese by birth, but they had lived among us for years. They had chosen wives from our people. Their children were in our schools. They wouldn't do us any harm.

Only later did we find that during the long years of their residence among us some of them had been busy sending vital information about roads and bridges and the training of reservists to the Japanese consulate in Manila. Only when the Japanese moved in to set up a government did we learn that one of these men had actually led the troops through the hills to Bontoc, and that another was a graduate of an engineering school in Japan and held a high rank in the Japanese Army.

The children of these Japanese were the most to be pitied. They thought of themselves as Igorots. Their education in our schools was that of any Filipino, with a strong bias in favor of American history and American culture. And now they had to adjust to the fact that the homeland of their fathers was at war with their native country.

There was one particularly sad case. One of the Japanese had a son and a daughter; Marcos was in his 20s, and his sister was in her teens. She was a pretty girl and when the invading army moved in she was immediately apprehended and put to work "entertaining" the troops. Her brother seethed, but was unable to do anything to help his unfortunate sister.

Marcos, when questioned by the Japanese command, told them that he had not gone south to join his Filipino outfit because his sympathies were with Japan. Actually his father, who had been interned by the Filipino authorities and then removed to a distant camp, had extracted a promise from him that he would take care of his sister until such time as the father was released from custody and could resume his guardianship.

Marcos was a good driver, and the Japanese soon put him to

work chauffeuring officers to and from Baguio. Despite the breaks in the roads, the Japanese maintained a system of transportation, in some cases having to drive to an impassable obstacle, on the other side of which there awaited another car which had been sent out from that side of the obstruction. For several months Marcos ferried Japanese soldiers back and forth.

Then one day he learned that his sister along with a group of pretty young Filipinas had been sent to Japan, having been promoted to serve as prostitutes to Japanese officers. Marcos could scarcely contain his anger, but he managed to display an outward calm as he planned his vengeance. He was scheduled to drive a truck conveying about ten officers to a parley in Baguio. About halfway there, as he reached the top of a rise with a steep drop at the shoulder, he swerved suddenly and drove the truck over the side of the road to its destruction 100 feet below. There were no survivors.

At the outbreak of the war we had two guests from Manila in the Rectory. Robert Wilner, Suffragan Bishop of the District, had been making an official visit. Our other guest was Benson Harvey, the Canon Missioner whose parish was made up of American families engaged in lumbering, planting, and other businesses scattered all over the archipelago. He had been making his rounds in Northern Luzon when the war began, and he had stopped at our home on his way back to Manila.

Bishop Wilner told us that he would remain with us until the unpleasantness with Japan came to an end and he could travel safely back to Manila, but Father Harvey was determined to get back to Manila to join his wife and daughter as soon as possible. For a while he walked, thumbing an occasional ride with some of the few vehicles still operating in the north country. Then he "borrowed" an unattended bicycle he chanced to see alongside the road. By remaining out of sight in daylight and being especially cautious as he travelled at night, he eventually made his way back to his home in Manila.

In the hectic days following the initial landings of the Japanese, no one really seemed to know how to behave. I recall that a Protestant minister wanted desperately to try to reach the south in order to volunteer for service in the Corps of Chaplains. He was finally persuaded that this trip would be impossible. Instead he joined a small band of Filipinos who were determined to add to the growing number of guerrilla fighters.

Later, when we were in Camp Holmes in Trinidad Valley, I found his wife in the camp. I asked her about her husband, and she told me that he had been killed in action.

Then there was the man who held a commission in the U.S. Army reserves. When hostilities began, he buried his uniform and destroyed every paper which would have connected him with the

Army. I am sure he wasn't a coward. He just didn't know what course of action to take. He survived the war.

By this time, war hysteria had seized us all. Every sizeable community in time of war regards itself as being high on the list of enemy targets. We were no exception. Of course the Japanese would bomb Bontoc. Was not our town the capital of the province? Did we not lie at the junction of two roads? Was there not a legitimate military installation, the headquarters of the Philippine Constabulary for the northern end of the Province located in our town? So we had better prepare.

Someone in authority in Manila had commanded blackouts, which we at first carried out by draping heavy blankets over our windows at night. Later when those responsible for operating the power plant a few miles from Bontoc heard a rumor that the Japanese were advancing, they became frightened and abandoned their posts, leaving the town in a complete electric blackout from then on. But we still had candles and kerosene lamps which we had to shield at night.

I offered the town the concrete building housing the Girls' School and dormitory as an air-raid shelter. But it would have to be sandbagged at ground level if it was to withstand any concussion which might result from a dropped bomb. We had no sandbags. But we did have many bolts of cotton print which we had used to make dresses for the girls. and we had women who knew how to use sewing machines. As rapidly as the women stitched these fancy flower prints into the shapes of bags, willing volunteers rushed them down to the Chico River and filled them with gravel and sand, and then returned to the Mission compound where we stocked them around the foundations of the buildings.

As the days passed, we occasionally saw or heard high-flying planes, but never did one even dip down to see whether Bontoc was where the map indicated it should be.

We had time to make other preparations. We knew, for example, that combatants had to be distinguished from the general population by wearing uniforms, or they might be considered guerrillas and suffer accordingly if captured. But our Constabulary troop had moved out of Bontoc and had taken all their military uniforms with them. So we devised a simple uniform for the "Bontoc Volunteers" —blue denim bandoliers. We then passed word along by travellers going south and by phone as far as the disrupted communication system permitted, and by posting a notice on the bulletin board of the Provincial Capitol building that anyone so attired was to be regarded as a regular soldier and not as a guerrilla.

In the meanwhile, I carried on as normal a schedule as I could. I visited my outstation chapels and schools as frequently as possible, having to use my legs and a bicycle rather than an automobile, because we had so little gasoline.

Word reached me one day that the men of Tukukan, one of my stations, were showing a measure of inhospitality to refugees from the lowlands who were fleeing the Japanese and seeking safety in the mountains. Groups of lowland Filipinos trudging along the highway would reach the vicinity of Tukukan, and get no farther. Some of the men of that village were lying in wait for them, attacking them, and even reviving the head-hunting practices of the past.

With Albert Masferré, a newly ordained deacon from my first Seminary class, I hiked up to Tukukan and assembled the men of the village in an emergency meeting. I told them that I had become aware of what they were doing, and while, due to the war situation, I could not make a report of this to the government authorities, I was keeping a list of those taking part in the head-hunting, and unless the raids stopped at once, and they allowed refugees to pass through their territory safely, I would send this list to the authorities at the first possible opportunity.

I further demanded that they befriend the travellers insofar as they could by offering them food and shelter if they were in need of either. I asked them to give me their word that they would behave themselves. and when the village elders acquiesced and assured me that they would see to it that no further atrocities were committed, I showed them a list on which I had written some names, and then tore it up.

But now an unexpected problem arose and threatened to bring our mission activities to a halt. We were running out of money. With the Japanese between us and Manila, we had no means of replenishing our supply of cash. This problem was solved in the time-honored manner of governments everywhere—we printed our own.

The Mountain Province government had two million pesos on deposit in the National Bank in Manila. The Sagada Mission printing press had a small supply of distinctive bond paper. We turned out currency in various denominations, asserting on the face of these bills that they were redeemable after the war in the legal tender of the Philippines, and then carefully recorded the amounts and numbers of the currency thus produced. The Bontoc Mission gave promissory notes to the Provincial Treasurer for as much of the money as we felt we needed and then used it to pay our teachers and other mission workers.

Because it had the backing of the Mission, the script was freely accepted by tradesmen in the area, and thus commerce did not come to a standstill. We discovered much later, when we were prisoners of the Japanese, that the military police were furious that this currency had been produced because it had enabled the guerrillas who were carrying on operations in the area to purchase food and supplies with which to carry on their resistance. They made inquiries trying to discover who was responsible for the creation of this issue of currency, but the Igorots had little love for the Japanese who had stolen their animals, emptied their granaries and raped their women, so they gave as little information as they could when questioned about anything.

Had my name been associated with this enterprise, I would surely have been executed. I was already in considerable bad odor with the Japanese. They had my name on the list of those who had sent contributions to the Chinese cooperatives which sprang up all over occupied China after the invasion of that country by the Japanese in 1937.

In more peaceful days as I had travelled the narrow trails between Baguio, Bontoc, Sagada and the lowlands, I had often thought that one could defend the interior of the Province without the construction of elaborate fortifications. A few blown bridges here and there, an avalanche or two which might be triggered with a few dislodged boulders, or even the setting of brush fires where the precipitous trails passed through narrow defiles, and the task of defense would be accomplished.

And now that war had come, we saw that the employment of such measures did indeed take place. Long after the lowlands had been overrun, the Mountain Province remained free of invaders. American and Filipino demolition experts were sent into the Province by the disintegrating American forces to destroy bridges, bring down landslides and dynamite narrow roads which had been carved into the cliffs overhanging the forests and jungles far below.

We were still ministering to the people of the area, despite the difficulty of getting around. We were hoarding our small supply of gasoline against the possibility of having to make a long trip someday in better times, so we travelled almost exclusively by bicycle.

One day as I was pedalling furiously between Bontoc and Tukukan, I swept around a sharp turn and found to my horrified dismay that a little wooden bridge which should have carried the road across a deep gulch was no longer there. An engineer had been at work during the night. The bridge lay a mass of wreckage at the foot of the ravine. My bike and I joined these ruins with bone-jarring rapidity. The 20-foot fall stunned me, and left me ensnarled in the broken wheel of my conveyance. I was not badly hurt, but no matter how I struggled, I could not free myself from the tangled bicycle. So I simply lay there and bellowed for help.

It was at least 30 minutes before I heard an answering shout. The rescue party consisted of a frail little old woman, who picked her way down the precipitous bank of the gulch, and gravely disentangled me from the wreckage. She never smiled through the entire operation, nor had she any comment to offer on the ludicrous situation. Having effected the rescue, she scrambled up the bank and went on her way, with not a word, and quite as though it were perfectly normal to find an American priest in such a predicament.

Perhaps she was affected as the rest of us were by a sense of detachment. We all seemed to be waiting—for what we did not know—and in the meanwhile whatever we did, however serious, or ridiculous, was done as though it really didn't matter. Real life had ended on December 8, and this was a kind of nightmare, a fantasy. Soon we would all awaken and get back into the swing of things.

During this hiatus from reality our routine was interrupted by an unexpected visit. A young American Signal Corpsman who had been with his outfit some place near Aparri, far north in Luzon, staggered into Bontoc late in December. After Pearl Harbor and the simultaneous attacks on various Philippine installations, he became separated from his detachment while they were trying to work their way south to join other American Army units. Our friend who eventually reached Bontoc had plodded for days through flooded paddies, and over trackless hills through the wild reaches of Northern Luzon, avoiding the roads and trails in order to escape detection by the Japanese. By the time he reached Bontoc his feet were badly blistered and infected. We were not yet under Japanese occupation there, so I advised him to seek treatment at our Provincial Hospital.

This he did, and every afternoon Florence and I would walk up to visit him. His father was a stone-cutter back in the Pennsylvania Dutch country, and our friend amused himself during the long days of hospitalization by sketching designs of headstones. Some were simple and severe, and some were rococo and outlandish. All carried names of his many hometown friends and army acquaintances. He had even designed one for me. He explained that he tried to fit the type of monument to the character of the person as he interpreted it. I am glad to say that my stone was dignified and unostentatious in its design.

Perhaps that was because on our daily visits we always carried Joe a few tidbits and a little reading matter. One day when we reached his room he fairly leapt out of bed, and tossing the most recent loan, a detective story, down on his bedside table, he said, "Now sit down and tell me who did it."

"Can't you read it yourself?" I asked.

"How?" he demanded in disgust, riffling throughout the pages of the book he had meanwhile retrieved. Midway through the book the center of the pages had been cut out, leaving only the margins, so as to create a little pocket, invisible when the book was shut. It was the bank of my bachelor days. I had fashioned the hole to have a hiding place for currency which I did not want to leave in my desk. I had long since stopped using it and had forgotten it.

I had not created the bank because of distrust of my houseboys.

100

On the contrary, it was because they were so honest, in those happy days before they met hordes of Americans during World War II. One day after I had been on a three-day trip I remembered that I had left a stack of 100 one-peso bills in plain sight on my desk near an open window. (It was the dry season and there was no need to fear any showers.) I put the spurs to my horse and hurried back. I rushed into my study and there was Jacob, my houseboy, sitting on the floor near the desk, with his eyes riveted on the currency.

"Oh, Jacob," I said, "I was afraid that money might be stolen!"

"Oh, no, Apo Padi," he said, "no one could steal it for I have been in this room ever since you left three days ago. I have been watching it."

"And haven't you gone to school?"

"No, Father, and Carlos has brought me my food and has helped me watch the money."

"But, Jacob," I protested, "why didn't you just open the drawer there and put the money in it?"

"You have told me, Apo Padi, never to touch anything on your desk."

American G.I.'s have complained that their experiences with Filipinos were far different. What they forget is that for several bitter years the Filipinos, as a subjugated people, were victimized by the Japanese occupying forces. They had to take advantage of every opportunity which came their way to survive those years. The pre-war Igorot was usually as innocent as little Jacob, anxious to please, and free of guile. My mutilated book, therefore, was not so much a protection against dishonesty, as it was a device to spare the Igorot boys the bother of serving as watchdogs when I had cash in the house.

Joe had become interested in the detective story, and then, at a crucial point the book had become my bank. I did my best to recall the story and more or less reconstructed the plot over the next few days. Joe had the good grace to seem satisfied with my efforts.

He was still a patient when the Japanese invaded Bontoc. It wasn't until years later that I learned that as their soldiers walked into the front door of the hospital, loyal Igorot hospital orderlies carried him out the back door and hid him in an outhouse until they could find a family willing to shelter him until the Japanese left town.

During those early weeks of the war, we knew very little. Our only source of news was the Voice of Freedom, broadcasting from Corregidor, and the "news" sent out over the airwaves by that station was intended more as a boost to flagging morale than as accurate information. But we never lacked for rumors. We had them in all degrees of absurdity. Chinese troops had landed at

Aparri! The Pacific fleet had recaptured Guam and was making knots to Manila! Hundreds of American planes had raided Manila and the Japanese were leaving the Islands by every possible means!

It was good, indeed, that hope had never fled Pandora's Box. We lived on it.

CHAPTER XVI

The most persistent and only really credible rumor was that the Japanese were gradually penetrating the more remote sections of the Islands, and that soon they would be in Bontoc.

When, eventually, the report turned out to be true, it would be difficult to say who was the more frightened—they, the invading soldiers, deep in hostile territory and surrounded by tribesmen whose reputation for headhunting had been greatly exaggerated—or I, an enemy civilian trapped behind Japanese lines with a wife and two small children and absolutely no hope of making contact with our own forces. They bluffed to cover their fear, and I bluffed, because I, too, was terrified.

That day in January 1942 had been uneventful. I had gone about my business. I had visited the hospital. I had conducted classes in the school, I had made a few calls in the village. I had gossiped a bit in the town plaza. I had listened politely to the rumors that the Japanese would surely reach town that night, but in the absence of any confirmed reports that they had been seen any farther east than Cervantes, I had remained skeptical.

Late that evening a villager came rushing to the Rectory to report that he had come 15 miles from Sabangan, where earlier in the day he had managed to elude Japanese guards who had been posted around a small detachment of infantrymen. To him it seemed evident that the soldiers were only waiting for the heat of the day to pass before resuming their march to Bontoc.

Florence and I had discussed our course of action many times since the outbreak of war, but now that the nightmare of meeting Japanese soldiers face to face was on the verge of becoming a reality, we had many second thoughts about what to do. We repacked a box of food, made up chiefly of canned milk and baby foods for the children, and we fussed again and again over the contents of a single suitcase of clothing. Most of the items were diapers. Then, nervously, we waited.

Our blackout curtains were drawn, but periodically we peered out into the night. The white concrete church across the street reflected the brilliance of the full moon. Silver rays danced on the broad and gently swaying leaves of the banana plants in our front yard. Far off in the native village we could hear the dogs singing their mournful dirge to the impassive moon.

Then there was a single pistol shot, and a shout. Was it of warning or of anger? Japanese or Igorot? We could not tell. I quickly put on my clerical collar and cassock, and blowing out the flame of the kerosene lamp, I retreated to the bedroom upstairs. Florence was already stationed near a window in the pitchblack room. Joining her, I could see the compound flooded in moonlight, and the street in front of our house, like a pale ribbon, leading up to the main highway.

We hadn't long to wait. A squad of heavy-booted men jogged in double time down the street and quickly took up positions outside our garden gate. In other circumstances the play of moonlight on their rifle barrels, fixed bayonets and steel helmets would have been fascinating. Now it was terrifying.

But they, too, were frightened. The two-story house was in darkness. They didn't know what dangers lurked in its interior, or in the clumps of coffee bushes, gardenia plants, and other heavy foliage which surrounded the house.

On a command from the leader of the squad, several soldiers detached themselves from the group and advanced stealthily into the shadows cast by the house, poking vigorously into the shrubbery with bayonets. Others levelled their rifles at the blackened windows, while the sergeant, flanked by two of his men came to the front door and called out loudly and ferociously in Japanese.

One didn't have to be a linguist to know that he "wanted in." Cold sweat broke out on my forehead as I tried, with all the courage I could muster, to walk quickly down the single flight of stairs. But my knees were shaking so that it seemed to take me forever to reach the lower level. By that time the soldiers had used their gun butts and had broken through the bolted door.

One of them seized the flashlight from my hand, and with its searching beam located one kerosene lamp in the living room and another in the office. These they lighted. In the meantime they had pushed me against the hall wall and had pinned me there with a bayonet pricking my Adam's apple.

"Espy-u!" hissed the sergeant. "American-u espy-u!"

"American, yes," I heard a strange quavery voice reply. "American! But not spy! No! Priest, teacher, missionary, Christian," went on the voice, which as it spoke lost some of its tremor and came to sound more and more like my own. "Spy, no!" I repeated, shaking my head as vigorously as the bayonet blade which still rested against my throat would permit.

"Den no espy-u, why for you here?" asked the soldier.

"I live here," I replied, "Why for YOU here?"

This bit of temerity was a mistake. The only reply was a sharp smack on my face, and another sibilant "Espy-u!"

Meanwhile the soldiers were rifling my desk and looking into drawers and closets for some evidence of my espionage activities. The soldier who had me pinned to the wall with his bayonet pricked a little harder, while the sergeant continued to say "espy-u!", slapping me occasionally.

Suddenly I became aware that their interest had been diverted from me. Florence had come down the stairs. She moved into the little circle of light, pushing gently through the soldiers. To the folds of her dressing gown clung a terribly sleepy little girl, our two-year-old Penny, and in her arms was nestled Jane, six months old.

"Baby!"

"Pletty American-u baby!"

"Ah, boot-iful baby!" The Japanese soldiers were cooing like women at a christening as they crowded around the mother and little girls. The soldier who had been guarding me joined in the group admiring the children, and for the first time in those eternal minutes, I found I could swallow without the risk of cutting my throat.

Taking instant advantage of their interest, my clear-headed wife addressed the soldiers as though they had been old friends who had just dropped in for a casual visit.

"You. Japan. Baby?"

Unfortunately, none of the soldiers spoke English.

"You. Nippon. Baby?" This time she pointed to our own children and to us, and then to them with an inquiring expression on her face.

One of the brighter men caught on.

"Ha! Ha! You Nippon baby," he affirmed and with great haste he reached into his tunic pocket and pulled out a wallet from which he extracted pictures of a little Japanese woman and several toddlers. A great clatter of rapid-fire Japanese ensued as each man laid his rifle down and went rummaging through his pockets for similar snapshots of his own children. Then, as men will everywhere, they talked among themselves, I supposed of the beauty and cleverness of their own children.

One of the soldiers had been chucking Jane under the chin, and when she awoke and yawned, he quickly reached into his pocket and shoved a piece of candy into her mouth. I saw it not as a piece of hard candy, but as a magnet for every germ between the Equator and the Tropic of Cancer, so I instinctively reached into her mouth and retrieved it. Rather than further offend this soldier who no doubt had been carrying this hardball around for a special occasion for some time, I popped it into my own mouth, letting him think me more greedy than ungrateful.

This small looting party of frightened young men obviously had no clear purpose in mind. When they became convinced that I was not dangerous, they left me alone while they systematically went through my desk in the study. I am quite sure they could not understand enough English to know what they were looking for.

I had on top of my desk a pile of papers representing ten years work. It was a translation into Lepanto Igorot of the Gospel according to St. Matthew. In compiling it I had had the assistance of Edward Longid and Albert Masferré, two of the three lads in my first class in the embryonic Seminary. So that it might be useful in some of the outlying areas of the region where the vocabulary differed slightly, I had sent copies out to other educated men for their comments and suggestions. Unfortunately, all of the copies had been returned and were on my desk.

I had planned to send the manuscript to the American Bible Society within a few days. However, the disruption of mail service due to the rapidity of the Japanese advance had prevented me from doing so. Now our unwelcome visitors picked up the manuscript and tore it to shreds, tossing the pieces into a knapsack one of the men was carrying.

Many other letters and papers suffered the same fate. Although they peered into a closet and under furniture, they failed to notice a Moro kris which I had hung on a nail behind the front door, with instruction to Florence that she should not hesitate to use it in a case of dire necessity. (Although we had numerous Japanese visitors while the looters were in town, not one of them ever noticed our weapon.)

But their leader did demand, in gruff tones, that I turn over to him my camera. I reached into the closet and brought forth an inexpensive box camera. He glared at me, threw the camera on the floor and stamped it under his heavy boot, shouting "No! German camera!" How he knew I had an expensive Leica I do not know, but he did, so I reached behind a box on the shelf of my closet and produced it. He nodded and put that into the knapsack which now contained the papers which had been on my desk.

After a few more hasty glances into closets the men were satisfied that I had nothing of further interest. Meanwhile, while those soldiers not engaged in rifling my desk and stealing my camera were still entranced with the children, I had been thinking. On the other side of the street was a little cottage in which lived Miss Gladys Spencer, a missionary who had spent many years in Aomori, Japan, and who had been "lent" to the Philippine Mission when Americans had been ordered out of Japan. I knew that if I could get them over there, she with her fluent Japanese would be able to straighten out much of this unpleasantness.

"Nippon-go. Woman. You. Me. We go?" I repeated this without success several times, and with variations only in the order of my words. Even though I pointed to the cottage on the other side of the street, my words met with only uncomprehending stares. (Wars between people having a common language must be much easier to wage.)

A flash of inspiration prompted me to try again. "Nippon-go, woman, Aomori (the name of the city where Miss Spencer had lived). Come?" I asked, having increased my Japanese vocabulary by 100%. Whether it was the addition of the name "Aomori" or the fact that I gently prodded the sergeant in the direction of the door, I don't know, but this time it worked, and we all went out into the night in search of Miss Spencer.

She, in the meanwhile, had been trying to keep her eye on the Rectory and on the wanderings of several soldiers who had been getting a little too close to the girls' dormitory. As we came to her garden gate, she came out to meet us, and bowing in Japanese style from the waist, she said in fluent Japanese, "You are soldiers of great Japan?"

"Hai!"

"Then you must be weary, for you have come a long way. Do come into my humble cottage and rest."

With one accord they looked at their filthy campaign boots, and at her nicely polished porch steps. Hearing their own language reminded them of their manners, apparently, for their leader replied in Japanese which Miss Spencer interpreted for me, "Oh, you are so gracious, but our feet are very dirty and we cannot soil your clean floors. Perhaps another time."

From then on until the time of their rapid retreat several weeks later when some guerrilla fighters frightened them away, our relations with these Japanese were tolerable, for Miss Spencer was always on hand to serve as translator.

It was through a friendly Japanese resident of Bontoc, one of our parishioners, that we learned some time later that these few soldiers who moved in on that first night had been scared to death of what they might find in the hills of Luzon, that their cartridge belts were empty save for gravel, and that the only live ammunition possessed by anyone in their party was a few rounds for the sergeant's pistol. But their bluff had worked. They had successfully intimidated the remnants of the Philippine Constabulary, the residents of all villages along their line of march, the priest-in-charge of the Bontoc Mission, and everyone, in fact, except Florence and Miss Spencer.

It remained for a later group of soldiers who confiscated my house for use as a residence for their commanding officer to clear the shelves in my study of more than a thousand volumes and to pile them up on the lawn and set them afire.

We had heard so many tales about the looting and unruly conduct of the advancing Japanese columns that, before they reached Bontoc, I had constructed a hard wood chest, painted it with cre-

107

osote and sealed the seams with wax. Into it I put my better ecclesiastical vestments and then buried it fairly close to my house. But alas, the termites did find a way of getting into the box, and when I excavated it after the first invaders had left us, I found nothing but a lot of rags. Those vestments which I had left hanging in the sacristy of the Church had not been disturbed. One never knows how to behave in the face of a hostile invasion.

For example, table silver which we had thrown over the back fence into a neighbor's yard, and which we really never expected to see again, was returned to me after the war. One of the tea pots had been punctured by shrapnel, but we have since mended it. However, my Bible translation and my library have been lost forever.

Shortly after the looting party had left us, an army jeep came to our house, and an officer stepped out and introduced himself as Captain Allen, the husband of Dr. Beulah Ream. He was an officer in the Philippine Scouts and the Scouts had been integrated into the U.S. Army. His mission on this trip was to check on the demolition work of engineers who had been sent north to destroy bridges and otherwise slow the advance of the Japanese. Before he left, he assured us that the enemy advance into the Province had been slowed considerably and with genuine concern he sympathized with us about the loss of so much of our food supply to the looters. He opened the back of his jeep and brought forth several loaves of bread. "I'll not need these, because I am heading back south now," he said.

We learned later when we found his wife, Dr. Ream, in the concentration camp, that he did return from that mission, only to be captured later. He then became the first of the hundreds to perish on the death march from Bataan to a prison camp.

CHAPTER XVII

Our visitors were a foraging party, and although they did not stay very long, their presence did nothing to endear the Japanese soldiers to the local populace. Too many hogs, too many sacks of rice, too many stores of precious food were carried out of the village to suit the Bontocs.

Day after day different soldiers, singly, in pairs, and in small groups, came to the Rectory and helped themselves to whatever they fancied. There was one exception. Whenever one tried to take a can of milk, I would smile and say, "No, *dozo* (please), for baby," and invariably the milk can would go back on the shelf.

Eventually word must have reached the officer in charge of the party that there was a veritable treasure house of canned goods at the Rectory. In a commandeered car, he was driven down to our front door and through an interpreter he explained to me that we were in Japanese-occupied territory, which had seemed rather apparent to me, and that therefore, since we were enemy aliens, our property belonged to the Imperial Japanese Army.

I told him that I had withheld nothing from his men except milk for the baby. He agreed that there had been no complaints about me, and therefore, out of the kindness of his heart, he proposed to confiscate only one half of my food for the use of his troops, leaving the other half for us to keep for our own use.

So that wandering soldiers would not molest us further, he handprinted a sign in bold Japanese characters advising all who might read it that the occupants of this house had voluntarily contributed half of their food to the Japanese army, and that no one was to demand any more of them. He signed it with his seal and nailed it to our front door.

Although our pantry was now off limits, we still had a lot of Japanese visitors. On our living room wall was a large mirror with Chinese soap-stone panels. The soldiers had passed word along in the barracks that they could see what several years of campaigning had done to them by looking at their reflections in this gorgeous mirror. They came, and invariably would go first to the mirror, and there admire themselves, stroking their beards and rearranging their mustaches, all the while joking with one another or with me, if one soldier had come alone.

One day I heard someone moving around in the pantry. He was shifting cans and bottles around obviously searching for something in particular. When I approached he said to me, in a gruff voice, "Whiskey!" When I said, "No whiskey," he dropped his voice and asked, "Wine?" Again I had to disappoint him. "Beer?" was his next, plaintive, question. "No whiskey, no wine, no beer!" I assured him. Then he spied a bottle of potassium permanganate which we used in dilute form for washing garden vegetables. He seized it and said, "Ah, wine!" Uncorking it, he raised it to his mouth and was about to gulp it down when I pulled it away from him. I certainly didn't want one of his buddies to find him writhing in agony in my house. "Poison!" I said, but that word wasn't in his vocabulary so as we struggled for possession of the bottle I remembered that these lads had been in combat in the lowlands and must surely have heard Filipino soldiers crying *"Patay!"* (death!) as they made their charges. I stuck my finger into the uncorked bottle, and pretended to suck it, and then simulating one in great pain I fell to the floor saying the one word which I knew would frighten him. He caught on, and after smelling the contents he threw the bottle on the floor in disgust. I gave the disappointed would-be tippler a few bananas and escorted him out of the house, relieved that I would not have to explain the presence of a Japanese corpse in my kitchen.

On another occasion a private appeared and told us that his lieutenant would be visiting our house within a short time and that we were to have a hot bath ready for him and three others. I told him in sign language and monosyllables that our hot water tank was small and we could furnish water for only one hot bath. With a smile of understanding he assured me that one water and four men would be a satisfactory ratio.

The lieutenant, two sergeants and a private appeared in due time, and in order of seniority climbed into the tub. When they had finished it looked as though a walrus had been splashing around in that room. But they did smell better when they left the house than when they had arrived.

The soldiers were homesick and quite eager to observe family life, even that of an American family. They never failed to show pleasure when they saw our little girls, and they frequently brought them gifts of candy, bricks of solidified soy sauce, and small quantities of tofu.

One day the private who had arranged the baths appeared with a pair of olive drab pants over his arm. "Belong to Lieutenant," he explained. "You will fix." The seat of the trousers was in shreds. My wife showed him the few pieces of material she had, none of which remotely resembled the hue of the trousers. He gravely examined the various samples and chose a piece of turkey-red cloth, which we used to make loin-cloths for our school boys. Florence was startled at his selection, but it was his choice, and she obediently patched the brilliant red cloth into the seat of the lieutenant's pants. I have often wondered whether it didn't make a tempting target for some American sharpshooter in the days when the tide of war had turned and the Japanese were fleeing through the mountains.

The townspeople and the villagers alike were getting tired of their guests, and somehow someone got word to a group of guerrillas hiding out in the hills nearby.

One day a Japanese patrol was ambushed, and the few survivors came running back to Bontoc with highly exaggerated stories of the strength of the attacking force. Our enemy quickly packed their loot and hastened south in confiscated vehicles.

We tried to resume our normal pattern of life. It was difficult. We had seen the enemy, and we did not like what we had seen. There had been many reports of outrages committed in the village and around the countryside. Our own provisions were down to almost nothing. Indignation ran high, and the townspeople vowed that they would not permit the Japanese to come into Bontoc again without a fight.

A few firearms were brought out of hiding, and various groups of Igorot warriors volunteered to stand off any soldiers with their spears and headaxes, but reliance for the most part was placed in the topography of our region. Rocks were poised precariously over the trails, and at a given signal, they were to be dropped on whatever might be on the highway below. Patrols ranged out of Bontoc daily to bring back reports of any troops moving toward us.

None came until May of 1942, and when they came, they entered the town with not a shot fired or a stone hurled. They walked in completely surrounded by American prisoners of war, captured in Bataan and Corregidor. These were among the few who had survived the infamous Death March. Even as they neared Bontoc, several fell by the roadside and died, to be buried sadly and reverently by the compassionate Igorots, who, in some cases, died themselves for giving succour to the Americans.

With columns of emaciated and staggering P.O.W.'s completely surrounding them, the Japanese were able to move in safety. This time they meant business. They were there to set up a military occupation. The Chinese Bazaar on the main street attracted the attention of the soldiers, and within a few moments it was an inferno. Houses were closely packed in that part of the *poblacion* and the flames roared from building to building, even blistering the paint on the back of the Rectory. In the meanwhile, one of the officers had made a quick appraisal of the situation and decided that my two-story Rectory would make an ideal command post, so he ordered his men to fight the advancing flames.

With only a half-inch garden hose, and a few buckets, it was a hard fight. As much water was poured down my Rectory walls from the bathroom faucet and out of the second floor windows as was thrown on it from outside. Miraculously, the fire was stopped before it could engulf our house, so, until we were hauled away from Bontoc, we did have our own home in which to stay.

I was summoned to the officer-in-charge of the occupying party the next day.

"You are the priest-in-charge?"

"I am."

"There are other missionaries in Besao, and Sagada, and Balbalasang?"

"There are."

"You will send word to all of them that they must be down here in Bontoc by Sunday afternoon, three days from now, or you will be shot."

"But how can I command these others? They are not in my jurisdiction."

"They will be here, all of them, or you will be shot."

"But I cannot possibly get word to Balbalasang. It is three days away and the missionaries there may have long since left their stations."

"Very well. I will excuse you from that responsibility. But the missionaries in Sagada and Besao will be here Sunday afternoon, or you . . . "

". . . . will be shot. Yes, I know. I will try."

I received permission to send fleet-footed messengers to my colleagues in Besao and Sagada. The communications they carried repeated the gist of my conversation with the Japanese commanding officer.

I was much relieved on the following Sunday to see a long column snaking in single file down the foot trail from Sagada. More than two dozen Americans and over a hundred Igorot porters and friends, laden with sacks of food, bedding and personal luggage made up the procession.

My ten years of work among these people had not been a "holding action," I realized as I saw among them Father Longid, our first ordained Igorot priest. To him had been entrusted the administration of the Sagada station, but he had come down to Bontoc to see if there was anything he could do to help. The only other priest from among the people whom we had taught at that time was the Reverend Albert Masferre, and it was to him that I committed the responsibility for the care of Bontoc. During the years of our incarceration, these two young men took over tasks formerly performed by two dozen people. They not only kept the work going, but actually made advances despite periodic spells in jail for questioning by the Japanese.

The following day we were all made to assemble in the plaza near the Provincial Building, where we were told that we would have to promise not to do anything hostile to Japanese interests. In return for our parole, we would be allowed to remain, for the time being, in the Mission buildings and in the grounds immediately adjacent, but, were told, except at church time, we could not gather in groups. Conversation with lowlanders or Igorots was denied us completely except for communication with Father Masferré and one other man who would do our marketing for us.

Should anyone in our party break these rules, I was told, my life would be forfeit.

I must have looked my feelings during those days, for one day a friendly fellow, a sergeant, I believe, called Florence to one side and warned her that her husband was glaring hatefully at the Japanese. This, he said, was not unnoticed by the Japanese, and they did not like it.

"You will tell your husband to hide his eyes, or he will be in serious trouble."

We knew that sooner or later we would be moved to a concentration camp for Americans in the Baguio area. The delay in effecting that move was due to the fact that the demolition engineers of the U.S. Army had done such a good job on the narrow road that no vehicles had as yet been able to get over the Mountain Trail. Out of respect for the white head of the eldest missionary in the party, Deaconess Massey, the Japanese told us they would not make us walk the hundred miles to Baguio but that we would have to be patient and await transportation.

One day, as I was sunning myself in the garden of the Rectory, I heard a loud "pssst!" On the other side of the wall was an Igorot friend from Alab, about ten kilometers south. He had a basket of fresh vegetables with him which he had brought as a gift for my family.

"How in the world did you get past the guards on the road with those?" I asked.

"Oh, several Japanese soldiers tried to take them from me," he said, but I told them thay the "would be naughty to take, because that would be stealing and God does not like stealing, and God does not like a stealer." Whether his admonition or his naivete had enabled him to keep his vegetables we shall never know.

So the Japanese came to stay—and with them came panic. Almost everyone connected with the government had fled to the mountains. Once again, Dr. Hilary Pit-a-pit Clapp stepped forward to serve his people. He refused to run away, feeling that he was needed in Bontoc. When the Japanese set about establishing a puppet government, their choices for a man to head it narrowed down to two, with Dr. Clapp first. Second was an upstart political malcontent who had collaborated with the Japanese by leading them into the heart of the province.

Dr. Clapp was in a quandary. He had maintained contact with several escaped American military prisoners, and he knew how desperate was their plight. Without relief packages from Bontoc, they would surely perish. He knew, too, that soon the Japanese would imprison all the American missionaries and that they, too, would be needing a friend on the outside. He also knew that the propaganda bureau had already started its campaign to wean the Igorots away from their loyalty to America. Yet he knew that as puppet governor, his own loyalty to America would be suspect, and upon the return of the American forces, which event he never doubted would come, it would be difficult to clear his name with them.

His dilemma was the more difficult because it seemed that the alternate candidate would truly serve the Japanese, and might do much harm to the allied cause. Hilary prayed. He conferred with me, his pastor. I told him that the decision must be his alone, but that if he did decide to play the part of a puppet, we of the mission would do our utmost to clear his name at the end of the war. He prayed some more. At length he looked over his shoulder, as he knelt, and said to me, "I shall serve my people. Please pray for God's blessing upon me."

From my house he went to the Japanese commandant's office, which had since been moved to another building, to accept the appointment.

For three years he served as governor. For three years he was in a strategic position which permitted him to send advance warning of military activities into the hills to warn the guerrillas of impending Japanese attacks. For three years, while he entertained Japanese officers in his parlor, relief packages were being prepared by his wife in their kitchen for the guerrilla soldiers in the hills.

Whenever suspicion arose due to the known fact that he had travelled in America and had been a friend of Americans, Dr. Clapp would on the next public occasion make bombastic speeches urging the people to turn to the Japanese as their friends. Such rhetoric seemed to satisfy the invaders.

Every time he went to Manila on government business, he succeeded in evading his guard long enough to pick up from the Bishop or from loyal Chinese Christians, money which he sent by devious routes into the internment camp at Baguio.

When the Americans invaded Luzon, and General Yamashita's beaten army retreated into the mountains, Dr. Clapp's position became precarious. He was urged by those who knew the role he had been playing to flee while there was yet time. But he knew that if he did this, he would leave behind many friends and relatives who would be unable to get away, and that the wrath of the Japanese

114

would fall upon them.

One day a band of guerrillas who knew nothing of the undercover work in which the doctor had been engaged raided the town. They captured him. Although he tried to explain the situation, they chose to take it at its face value. So far as they could see, they were arresting a collaborator. There was no one there to set them straight. On the way to guerrilla headquarters, one of the troops, no doubt believing that he was saving the government the trouble of a trial, shot and mortally wounded the doctor. He died on the trail, and was buried alongside the road.

In the meanwhile, we who had been interned had at the first possible moment filed affidavits with the office of the Provost Marshall in Manila testifying to the facts of the case. We had thought that these might still reach the mountains before the guerrillas did. Not until several months later did we learn that we had lost our race to vindicate our friend and benefactor.

Because of these affidavits, however, and because of evidence gathered by investigators into the sad case, in November 1946, the Third Guerrilla Amnesty Commission, meeting in Bontoc, concluded an exhaustive document relating all the facts in the case with these words: "It may be concluded that if Dr. Hilary P. Clapp was executed by the guerrilla organization . . . . the execution was a fatal mistake, for the late Dr. Clapp was a patriot and not a collaborator . . . "

The story of his heroic life of self-sacrifice, culminating in martyrdom, will long be remembered by the Igorots of Luzon. All Saints' Mission Church today possesses a handsome missal inscribed: *To the Glory of God, and in Loving Memory of Hilary Pit-a-pit Clapp, Christian and Patriot."*

Several weeks after all of the missionaries had been gathered on our compound, the friendly little interpreter sneaked into our house one night to give us advance warning that we would be moved to the Concentration Camp near Baguio the next day.

"The orders have come through," he said, "but the captain will not tell you until half an hour before you must leave. I think this is unfair. In that way he knows that you will have to leave many things which you might otherwise be able to pack. You will be allowed one bed roll for each person, and one suitcase for each adult. Perhaps by telling you now, you will be able to prepare."

We did, indeed, appreciate his advance warning, which we passed on immediately to the other Americans. We spent the greater part of the night packing and repacking our few allowable pieces, and making frequent trips to the back wall of the garden to toss silver and other valuables over to an Igorot neighbor.

The Captain's orders came through, as and when predicted, and at the appointed time we were escorted to the trucks and clambered aboard. The road was packed solid with our friends, and there were few dry eyes as we took our leave. Even at this dismal moment they were trying to cheer us up. One of the teachers, supposedly helping to arrange the load in the truck, whispered to me that a radio in town had picked up news of a tremendous naval victory for America in the Coral Sea off Australia. He was hazy as to details, but he assured me that it meant that the war would be over within a few weeks.

I wanted to believe this, too. I don't know how we could have maintained a semblance of cheer as we waved farewell had we known that none of these buildings would be standing when next we saw All Saints' Mission, and that it would be nearly a quarter of a century before we would see these familiar scenes and these friendly faces again.

But mercifully, the future is veiled from our eyes, so we stood in the truck, shouting that we would soon be back. It was not without pride that I waved farewell, for there in the crowd I could see two Igorot priests, men I had trained, and men who formed the vanguard of a great throng of ordained men who would rise from within the Philippine Church, to take over the places which Americans had been occupying since 1902. The task for which I had come to the Philippines in 1931 was well started. That I knew, and it was comforting.

CHAPTER XVIII

Travellers generally agree that one of the most spectacular mountain highways in the world is that connecting Baguio and Bontoc, but none of us, crowded into that Japanese army truck carrying us to the concentration camp which was to be our home for the next thirty months, had eyes for the magnificent scenery.

A Japanese infantryman lay prone on the roof of the cab, steadying himself by hanging onto a machine gun which had been riveted in place. He kept peering into the woods. Another soldier was stationed at the back of the truck, his gun pointed out over the tailgate. Still a third sat among us, with his automatic weapon on his lap. It wasn't hard to guess what his orders were should we be ambushed by guerrillas. So, we, too, watched apprehensively as we passed scores of places which might have concealed men bent on liberating us.

The only passenger who was completely comfortable mentally and physically during the whole trip was our little Jane. She was about ten months old. We were carrying her in a wicker market basket.

Due to the efficiency of American demolition engineers who had passed that way, and to the inefficiency of Japanese engineers who had been given the assignment of repairing the damage, the road was still in bad shape. Because the Japanese were not at all sure that a fully laden truck would be able to cross damaged places safely, we had to go afoot across numerous rickety bridges and bad stretches of road. Then we had to line up for a head count before climbing aboard the truck again.

Every time it was the same. The sergeant had a little notebook which apparently contained the names of all his charges. He didn't attempt to call the roll of those formidable western names, for they would surely have overtaxed his linguistic skill. Instead he merely passed along the single file, counting out, "one! two! . . . twenty-nine! thirty! thirty-one! . . . Ha! One missing!" He and his men would look anxiously back to the road we had just traversed. Much muttering was followed by a second count. "Twenty-nine! thirty! thirty-one! . . . ," and Florence, having let them stew for a few minutes would then say, "And here is thirty-two," pointing to our child sleeping in the basket she carried.

"Hokay! Get back!"

Off we went to the next bad stretch in the road, where we went through the same procedure. Our sergeant never once on that trip remembered little Janie tucked away in her basket.

None of us had any accurate information as to our exact destination. We had heard all sorts of garbled reports from Igorots who had been in Baguio about the nature of the American concentration camp, but these accounts had been so highly colored by the prejudices of the narrators that we had chosen to ignore them.

We were relieved, therefore, and somewhat startled, to find ourselves being driven into the Philippine Constabulary camp in Trinidad Valley, some ten kilometers north of Baguio itself. We knew this would be a far better location than the grounds at Brent School or the Pines Hotel or Camp John Hay, all of which had been used at various times to house internees of the Baguio region.

It was with many a whoop and holler that we were welcomed by the other internees when the truck came to a halt in front of a long low barracks building. We were among friends again albeit they, too, were prisoners. It was with special joy that I became an inmate of the camp, for now my responsibility for the good behavior of the missionaries who had been herded together on our compound in Bontoc came to an end.

The camp had been in existence for nearly six months prior to our arrival. Things were well organized. The Japanese permitted the Americans to conduct the internal affairs of the camp, and our captors dealt only with the camp committee. This was made up of men chosen in a general election conducted by the prisoners.

At the "processing" desk that first day, we all stated our special skills, preparatory to being assigned to various jobs. Most newcomers, even though they might claim technical knowledge which could have been useful in the shop, or kitchen, or hospital, found themselves on the dishwashing squad. Washing greasy dishes with no hot water, and only a limited amount of soap, was not a pleasant task. Once one became a "pearl diver" he was likely to remain at that job until he reported sick with dysentery. This disease, both of the amoebic and the bacillary varieties, was endemic in the camp, and sometimes, if a carrier in the food or dish handling department was not detected soon enough, it became epidemic.

We were also assigned our sleeping space—a bit of floor 5' x 7'. Families were not permitted to remain together. Men and older boys lived in one barracks. Single women, girls, and married woman without children were in another. The third barracks was the real madhouse. It was there that the younger mothers with small children lived.

Until the arrival of the 32 Episcopal missionaries, discipline in the camp had been puritanic. Cohabitation by man and wife was strictly forbidden, although love did often find a way. Several babies were born during our almost three years of camp life. But even co-mingling, as our captors called ordinary socializing between the sexes, was also forbidden. Except for an hour on Sunday, it was only through a barbed wire fence that men and women might communicate. That hour on Sunday—how we looked forward to it!

But we Anglican men pretended to be awfully dumb. We had not known the camp in its early months when the Japanese were really tough, so we constantly violated the rules by running over to the women's dorm to deliver or pick up laundry or to play with the children, or for any one of half a dozen other reasons. Then, if caught by the guards, we would mutter "So sorry, please," and stay right where we were.

Others saw that our blocks were not being knocked off, so they too began to bend and finally break the rules against co-mingling. Soon the regulations were universally ignored and from dawn until curfew we were reunited as families.

There was even a certain amount of undercover work going on at night, and most of the women were good enough sports to help their sisters in durance vile entertain their husbands by volunteering to babysit for children who might otherwise have been in the way.

In another way our arrival in camp helped to lighten the burdensome restrictions which had prevailed. With the Bontoc delegation the camp now held a bishop and seven priests, as well as half a dozen nuns. Up until our arrival there had been only the general Protestant service on Sunday mornings.

Now we asked for permission to have a celebration of the Holy Communion each Sunday, and for a place where we might conduct it. To our astonishment, permission was granted and the Japanese commandant even gave us a bottle of sacramental wine. He also told us that we might have a shack which had been used as a goat shed for our chapel, so we moved that to the end of the parade ground, spruced it up, and eventually it became an Anglican-Roman Chapel and a primary grade school room for the school which the camp committee, now emboldened by the new laxity at the guard house, organized.*

Ours would have been a good school anywhere. We had no end of talent, for the entire faculties of several secondary schools and even more primary schools were incarcerated in Camp Holmes. A survey showed that there were inmates who could offer instruction in several Chinese languages, Japanese, almost any European language, and all the classical languages, including Hebrew and Coptic.

---

*The commandant, at that early stage of our internment was Captain Tamibe, and he was truly civilized. His wife was a Christian, and he tried to make life as bearable for us as war and constant shortages of food would permit. Still, we were astonished to learn that he attended a reunion of camp survivors in San Francisco in 1981. He died a few years after that.

Furthermore, all branches of mathematics, including calculus, practically any of the sciences, as well as most of the more usual subjects that appear in high school and college catalogues could be taught by our fellow prisoners.

Our school graduated a good many youngsters, who, when they reached the States, were able to get with no difficulty into the colleges of their choice. One, David Bergamini, was admitted to Dartmouth and he later became a Rhodes Scholar, and the author of several learned books. The only real difficulty was the lack of textbooks, laboratory equipment, and paper.

But in solving this, we also managed to eliminate another problem. The Japanese gave permission for us to import old scrap paper from schools in the Baguio area. Old paper, used on only one side, began pouring in. What the Japanese did not know was that many of the math and chemistry problems so casually scratched on one side of the scrap were actually coded messages, previously worked out by camp inmates when they had had permission to go to the school to secure materials, and that these codes carried the latest war bulletins gathered from BBC and Voice of Freedom broadcasts.

We also had other sources of information. On his return from one of his licensed trips to the Baguio hospital for medical supplies, our medical officer had smuggled in a small radio. Then there was "Smitty." He was a radio technician. The Japanese knew this and employed him to keep the radio in the guardhouse in good repair. "Smitty" took hours to make the simplest repairs, during which time he carefully monitored all the BBC broadcasts he could tune in. Each time he was called to fix the guard's radio, he would make the repair, then leave a few drops of acid on thin wires in the instrument so that within a few days another visit to repair the burned out wires would be necessary. Our fourth source of news was a courier system. The garbage had to be carted out to a dump about one kilometer up the road. While the garbage crew was hauling the cart, they usually managed to pick up scraps of paper discarded along the road by friendly Filipinos who had received news from the guerrillas operating in the area. The news would then be whispered to trusted internees bending down close the foliage which concealed the natives.

It was because I helped spread these reports that I came close to torture and possibly death.

The Japanese Military Police were aware of the fact that news was getting into camp. Somehow they learned the names of some of those involved in circulating the information. A number of our men were taken out of camp, one at a time, and interrogated at police headquarters. One was killed while being questioned, and several others were brutally beaten. A favorite method of torture was to force the prisoner to drink great quantities of water, then beat him on his abdomen with clubs, fists, or boots.

One day, Gene Kneebone, one of those who had been taken for questioning, but who had survived the experience, told me that he had seen a list of men who were selected for questioning on the desk of the officer in charge of the investigation.

"Your name, Cliff," he said, "is the next one on the list. You'll probably go out tomorrow."

I was thunderstruck. Actually I knew nothing except that Father Sheridan, a member of the Maryknoll Missionary Society, occasionally gave me news reports which I passed along to a few friends. Where they originated in the first instance I did not know, and in such a situation it was good not to know too much. But now, apparently, I was to be questioned under torture.

I quickly concocted a wild tale about a former houseboy having been picked up for theft by the Baguio police, and told Florence that I had received word that I might be required as a character witness for the lad. I didn't think she believed the yarn, but she didn't pry any further, and simply said that she hoped that I would be back soon.

That night the Japanese guards delivered one of our internees to the hospital, painfully beaten. Under torture he had cracked and told the Japanese the little he knew, which merely confirmed information they already had. He was then given a few more blows to remind him to behave himself and was sent back to camp. With the information he had given, the Japanese were content and called off the investigation.

The Japanese did not seem to be very bright about intercepting or counteracting news that came to us from the outside. The classic illustration of their lack of competence in this area was probably the occurrence in Santo Tomas Internment Camp in Manila. A confirmed report that the Americans had landed in Leyte had been received and needed to be relayed to all the prisoners in the camp. The person who was permitted to make announcements on the public address system that day fabricated and broadcast a story of how the Japanese had finally consented to put a certain kind of vegetable on the menu. This dramatic bit of information was followed by the statement that while this concession had been long overdue, it was "better Leyte than never."

Our Igorot friends were not unmindful of our needs behind the barbed wire. On special occasions they were permitted to send in food baskets. On our first Christmas in camp, the women of the Church of the Resurrection in Baguio roasted dozens of chickens and brought them in, one for each missionary family member. Having a wife and two children, I was entitled to four, so there were several nonmissionary inmates who shared our good fortune on that day.

When it came to Christmas gifts, all of us learned to improvise. For weeks and even months before the holiday we would pick over the various junk piles here and there, or keep our eyes riveted to the ground for any scrap of anything which might be turned into a trinket or a gift. For example, old electric wire made curlers, bobby pins, and hairpins for Milady. A particularly symmetrical pine trunk which might ordinarily have gone into the firewood heap would be sliced carefully to form wheels for a cart for the kiddies. Tire treads with scraps of canvas to serve as thongs made slippers or shoes. Coconut shells and bones from the soup pot could be fabricated into novelty jewelry. Bottles rescued from the garbage pile, tin cans, and discarded aluminum pots, relics of fatter days, could be scrubbed and decorated and made into tableware or flower pots. Various vines and weeds were tough enough to be woven into belts. Anyone with a knife could whittle toys, clothes pins, forks, or spoons. The children were great scavengers. They would retrieve every bit of metal or glass they could spy out and gleefully seek out Daddy with the plea to "make something for me."

It was not until after we were released that we found out that many of our Filipino friends suffered dreadfully for trying to succor us. Many of them, attempting to pass information along to us, or to send us money for our relief, were caught, warned or imprisoned, and at least two that I know of paid with their heads for repeated offenses.

One of my first students was Benito Cabanban who became the first Filipino to serve as a Bishop in the Philippine Episcopal Church. He was a catechist in Upi, Cotabato, during the war. His father was a farmer. One day Benito Cabanban and his father were arrested and thrown into a military prison. They were not told of their alleged offense, but after several days they were dragged from their cell and led to the Church.

There the Japanese captain told them that they had just a few minutes to prepare themselves by prayer for their execution, for the offense of having given aid and comfort to guerrillas. The elder Cabanban declared that the charges were quite true, and that he had likewise given food and drink to Japanese soldiers who had stopped at his house.

"Our religion teaches us to be kind to those in need, and our Lord Jesus has told us to give food and drink to all whether enemy or friend. So this we have done. For this you have sentenced us to death? For what? For feeding the guerrillas, or for feeding the Japanese?"

The captain heard him out, and had the firing squad level their rifles at the father and son. Then, at the last minute, he dismissed the executioners and threw the Cabanbans back into their cell. A few days later they were brought before him again, scolded severely, ordered to have no further communications with the guerrillas, and released.

Edward Longid and his fellow priest, Albert Masferre, were imprisoned numerous times for the crime of "working for the American Church." These men also answered the charges by pointing out that they had been equally kind to Japanese and to Americans. They were usually thrashed, warned not to repeat their crimes, and released.

It was not the good fortune of military prisoners to be so tenderly handled. To the Japanese, by their code of Bushido, soldiers were disgraced by their capture, and were worthy neither of respect nor of humane treatment. Many were sent to notorious Fort Santiago in Manila, where most prisoners were either starved or tortured to death.

Despite the risk they knew they were taking, the Igorots continued to minister to us in the camp. They knew that we desperately needed money to buy extra food, and we would from time to time receive remittances to which only Igorot names were attached, names which were fictitious so that they could not be traced, but which the recipients were able to connect with episodes or people in the past. Whenever Dr. Clapp, while governor of the province under the Japanese, sent me money, it was designated as being from "Edna," and I knew the source for the doctor had a daughter by that name.

It was money remitted in this way that kept us alive. The Japanese permitted the camp to operate a small store. Lard, bananas, eggs, occasionally canned fish or meat, matches, cigarettes, leaf tobacco, and such items were sold by the Japanese or by authorized peddlers to store authorities and they in turn sold these items at cost to the internees.

It was usually possible, too, to do a little dickering with the guards. It was not unusual to ask a friend for the time of day only to have him reply, "I don't know. I ate my watch yesterday." Some of the guards wore several wristwatches on both wrists.

The bartering among the camp inmates was not only exciting, it also served as an indication as to current conditions in the camp. A premium price for cigarettes or light bulbs or flashlight batteries, paid in corn, or peanuts or beans or rice indicated that the Japanese were feeding us fairly well. However, let the exchange board advertise that coffee or tobacco or non-edible items were offered in exchange for food, and it probably meant the camp was being disciplined by the commandant for some infraction of the rules.

As the war dragged on the camp fare deteriorated. In the first year we had three meals a day, coarse and sparse, but sufficient to maintain a reasonable facsimile of health. Several times a week the Japanese sent in a tin garbage barrel of fish. By the time it reached us, after transit through the lowland heat, much of it had to remain in the garbage can.

At one time I was on the fish cleaning detail. It was a smelly job, but it had its advantages. Often we on the squad would retrieve a good fat strip of fish roe, too limited in quantity to go on the camp menu, which we would cook up for our own families.

As the months wore on, our ideas of what was edible changed. At first we had decapitated the fish just behind the gills, and cut off the tails at the end of the torso. Later, just before fish shipments ceased altogether, we were chopping off heads between the eyes and the mouth, and the tails remained where God had put them.

By the third year we were down to one meager meal a day, which would have been totally vegetarian had we depended solely upon the provisions offered by the Japanese. Only rarely did a piece of water buffalo or horse come our way. It was no wonder that the commandant's pet dogs disappeared if they ventured too close to the cook shed behind the men's barracks.

Under these conditions dysentery patients had an especially bad time. I was in the hospital twice. So were both of our little girls. The camp food was far too coarse for our ravaged digestive systems to tolerate, yet the ingredients of the bland diet necessary for recovery were expensive, if obtainable at all. The doctor told my wife that it was unlikely that she would be able to get all three of us home, and that she had better decide to whom she was going to give recuperative care.

Florence had never before broken down, but at this news, she sought out a place of solitude on the parade ground and sat down and wept. Father Robert Sheridan, the Maryknoll father to whom we had all become most attached, found her.

"Why the tears, Florence?"

She told him what the doctor had said.

"Well, well. I thought it was something serious," Bob said lightly. "Here is a hundred pesos," he said, peeling the bills off a roll, "and I can get more if you need it. You may return it after the war." This money, carefully hoarded by this good priest and augmented from time to time by delivery by circuitious routes against just such an emergency, was enough to enable Florence to buy the extra food we three needed to save our lives. This was the first debt we repaid when we returned to the States.

By the third year of internment many of us were losing weight at an alarming rate. We used to say that we needed to carry stones in our pockets to keep us from blowing away in the breeze, and that we had to sway from side to side at roll call to make sure the guards could see us.

The Japanese denied that the weight loss was serious. They laughed about it, but as a concession to our fears, agreed to keep a record of everyone's weight.

They brought in a well calibrated set of scales, and set up a table near the scales outside the barracks. Just before the first weigh-in, we all drank as much water as possible, refrained from visiting the latrine, put a little sand into our pockets, and wore any extra clothes we thought might detected. A soldier made notes of all names and weights.

A week later, prior to the second weigh-in, we were all careful to keep away from the water hydrants, we eliminated as much weight as we could, we wore our lightest clothing (most of us were in rags by this time anyway), and then stepped on the scales. The weight loss in each case: was so alarming that even our doubting commandant had to admit that we had a point.

However, he notified the internment camp's medical committee that in his opinion Americans, generally speaking, were unhealthily obese, and that we should be grateful to the Japanese army that we were no longer in that condition. He also declared that the rations allowed the prisoners were equal to those dispensed to the Japanese soldiers. What he failed to point out was that the soldiers had freedom to forage to supplement their rations.

In any case, there were no further weighing sessions.

Florence was the strong one of our quartet. Only once did she find it necessary to seek medical attention.

This was when her appendix became so bothersome that the doctor advised immediate surgery. Fortunately, there was still some spinal anesthetic available. However, there were no surgical sutures, so she was stitched together with ordinary cotton thread. It held, and apparently was absorbed into her tissues. Florence also suffered from malnutrition, for which no medical treatment was available. Because she was otherwise healthy, she had deprived herself of nutritious food in order to build up my strength and that of the children. She later told me that she was sure that God was keeping me alive to serve some useful purpose after the war. I have ever kept that in mind and I hope that my post-war ministry in America and South Africa justified her belief.

Our constant hunger was all the harder to bear because of our ignorance of what was happening at home. The Geneva Convention governing the care of prisoners in war time said that we were entitled to both incoming and outgoing mail at reasonable intervals. Although numerous letters reached the International Red Cross in Geneva for transmittal to us, very few of them got beyond Manila. I believe that during my 33 months of internment I received mail not more than three or four times.

And we found out later that not many of the monthly post cards the Japanese collected from prisoners for transmittal to our families at home ever reached them. They wouldn't have conveyed much information in any case. They were preprinted, with a few blank spaces which we were supposed to fill in. "I am interned in Camp Number three. I am being treated well and have good food. My health is (check one) excellent, good, fair. Please give my greetings to . . ." The one such card which finally reached my family did so weeks after they had received word of our liberation. From late in 1942 until we were released in 1945 they had feared that all four of us, including the two little girls whom they had never seen, had perished.

During these long months in the Trinidad Valley near Baguio our little cemetery on top of a hill overlooking the camp was steadily being enlarged. However, the graves there did not reflect our true mortality rate. The Japanese seemed to sense when a sick internee might be nearing the end of his ordeal. Such unfortunates were generally released on parole to the General Hospital in Baguio, or into the custodial care of friends. If they subsequently died, it was then no fault of the Japanese army, and it could not be chalked up as an internment camp death.

So, as food and supplies became scarcer and our resistance to disease became feebler, serious illness became more prevalent. Many of the ill refrained from reporting sick, for they knew there were no medicines, and they preferred the relative liberty of their own nooks and crannies in the barracks to the discomfort of the camp hospital.

While our physical condition worsened dramatically in the last year of our internment, our morale remained high. We knew that General MacArthur would be back, and the only question was which of us would be alive to greet him.

The Japanese permitted us to see their English language section of a Manila newspaper from time to time, usually when they fabricated some story of a big American set-back in the South Pacific.

The war accounts had a sameness about them that was ludicrous. American marines or soldiers assaulted an island. They were pinned to the beach. The fighting was furious and many American casualties were counted. The Japanese decided that the island had no strategic value. They withdrew. This clever ruse dispersed and neutralized many thousands of American fighting men.

As we followed these accounts we noticed what the Japanese apparently hoped we would not, namely that these American "defeats" were successively closer and closer to the Philippines.

The guerrillas became more active and bolder as the Americans got nearer. We were living in constant terror that they might attempt to liberate the camp. This could have resulted in slaughter in our ranks. Fearful lest some ill-advised guerrilla commander make an attack, and that in the resulting confusion families be separated with tragic results, many of us campaigned for permission to rearrange our housing to keep families together.

The champion of the "family plan," as it was called, was our friend and benefactor, Father Sheridan, a celibate. Father Sheridan had come into camp late, from a more comfortable internment experience in Manila. He knew that there were about forty Roman Catholics interned in Camp Holmes, including some Maryknoll sisters, but that they had no priest to minister to them. So, when it was suggested that a Roman Catholic priest might be allowed to go to the Baguio camp, Father Sheridan promptly volunteered. When he was elected to the camp committee, he was appointed chairman of internal affairs. So he quickly began a campaign to have the living quarters rearranged to permit families to live together.

At this point the deterioration of our mental processes became apparent. Old maids, cranky bachelors, and even some apparently happily married couples began protesting that family-unit living in camp conditions was impossible, that it was unnecessary, and that it would be immoral. Fortunately, they were in the minority.

The Japanese had maintained a benign neutrality during all the fussing, and had agreed to abide by the results of a referendum. The election was hotly contested, but the proponents of the family plan prevailed. The camp committee thereupon had to measure out all the square footage in the several barracks and to reassign space on the basis of the size of families.

I personally favored the plan, but its adoption made no difference in the Nobes' scheme of living for, on the appointment of Father Sheridan, I had occupied the post of Chief of Camp Police for several months prior to this. So that I might be available at any time of the day or night for any emergency which might arise, I had been assigned half of a detached 15' x 15' cottage for the use of my family. An English woman with three children occupied the other half, separated from our quarters by a sheet of woven bamboo and some blankets.

My chief duty as Police Chief was to guard the garbage cans to make sure that hungry internees did not filch any of the garbage. We needed it for our poultry and pigs, which we were hoarding against the day when meat rations from the Japanese would cease completely. Occasionally, I had to make surprise inspections of the personal effects of the prisoners to retrieve and place again in general circulation camp crockery and cutlery which had a way of disappearing with disconcerting regularity.

All of the ill-will which had been engendered during the "family plan" campaign might have been spared us had the Japanese given us information about the removal of the camp as soon as they had it themselves. However, with usual Japanese truculence, they withheld that news until the day after Christmas in 1944, when they told us that our camp was to be broken up and that we were to be moved to Manila the next day.

CHAPTER XIX

Although we suffered hunger, disease and occasional brutality during the 33 months we spent in Camp Holmes, our greatest trial was boredom. The daily routine was monotonous to say the least. Until close to the end of our detention, we were roused daily soon after sun-up for roll-call.

The women and children would line up before their dormitory and the men in front of theirs. When the Japanese soldier conducting the exercise was satisfied that the lines were straight, he would struggle through the roll call, shouting out the unfamiliar occidental names, to which we responded with a loud "here." Before he did this, we were expected to make a respectful bow in unison in reply to his morning greeting. The morning response was supposed to be "Hai-tai san, ohayo gazaimazu (Honorable soldier, good morning)." What was actually said when we bowed was generally far different, and unprintable in the memoirs of a man of the cloth. Roll call finished, there was a mad dash to the mess hall to line up again.

Some of the older and more feeble internees spent hours each day in line waiting for entrance to the dining room. They wanted to be among the earliest in, so that as soon as they gobbled down whatever the menu offered at that meal, they could leave the dining room and come back in for "seconds," if such were being offered, or to be at the head of the line for the next meal. These people usually had been excused from camp duties and could therefore spend their time on lines.

After breakfast we dispersed to various places to do our assigned tasks. The women took turns cleaning the rice, or corn, which was then boiled for meals. The quality of grain sent into camp by the Japanese quartermaster was such that it needed careful cleaning. Most of it was sweepings from granaries and carried much dirt, gravel, and insect life. At first the women picking the grain clean were careful to toss out that which had been infested by weevils. Later, the weevils were left in—protein was protein.

The squad of men assigned to take the garbage to the dump, approximately a mile from the camp, were envied by those with other tasks. Not only were these fortunates able to make occasional contact with Filipino civilians as they trudged along the highway, but sometimes a lenient guard would permit them to purchase bananas or other tidbits. And, of course, there was always the possibility that they might find a treasure, such as a discarded can or bottle or a length of wire at the dump.

A surly guard could make things awkward if he wanted to, but most of them were reasonable and allowed the men to retrieve such junk items.

Another privileged group was made up of those whose job it was to gather firewood for the kitchen stoves. They, under guard, of course, went to a nearby wooded area to chop down trees, which were then brought back to camp and left at the woodshed, where the trunks would be reduced to stove-sized sticks. They, too, had an opportunity to see Filipinos with whom they might barter or from whom they could sometimes get bits of news.

A third group that worked under the watchful eyes of guards were the gardeners. We attempted to grow some vegetables, but so often when the beans or other crops were ready to be harvested the guards would say, "So sorry, our vegetables delayed. We borrow yours and return later." Seldom were they returned. One of our most successful crops was the *camote*. These tubers had green tops, so their cultivation was doubly worthwhile. The Emperor of Japan to this day owes me ten kilos of this lowly vegetable. Men assigned to garden work were expected to put in a certain number of hours each day. In the third year of our camp, when food was very scarce, those who volunteered to work more than their required time were offered as a bonus an extra amount of camote. With a wife and two children in camp with me, I usually worked overtime, but while my hours were duly recorded in the log book, I never was given my bonus.

Other men served in various other capacities. There were seven medical doctors among the internees, and they took their turns in the dispensary and the hospital. Others from the general populace served as attendants in the make-shift facilities. Then there was a maintenance gang to keep the structures in shape, to attend to the plumbing, or to do whatever construction the Japanese allowed. The camp had a shop, equipped with basic tools, including a grindstone, a table saw, and such, which fabricated necessary items from materials salvaged by the garbage crew and those who occasionally were allowed to go to Baguio to dismantle some condemned structure. One of the members of the camp served as barber, another was the shoe repair man, a third acted as librarian, and still another was the electrician who produced miracles despite the shortage of wire, plugs and fuses.

Each internee was permitted to have a certain amount of floor area in the dormitories. But we soon had made agreements with one another through which the common living area serving a group of men became larger by combining bunks into doubledeckers, triple deckers and even a few quadruple deckers, firmly anchored to the floors and to the ceilings. This arrangement gave us more free floor space, which of course had to be furnished with homemade chairs, benches, tables and storage shelves. Nails were in short supply so many unions were made by using scraps of fence wire picked up by the garbage detail.

The kitchen gang was important, too. We were fortunate in that we had the chef from the Baguio Hotel with us. He did wonders with the limited materials on hand, so the food was usually edible, if not satisfying. The Japanese always made an "equal" division of the meat which was sent into camp. "Half" would remain at the guard house to feed the squad or two of soldiers and the other "half" would be sent to the kitchen to take care of the 500 prisoners. The soldiers assigned to butcher the animals would usually decide that the animal could be halved by sending us the shoulders, neck and head, while they kept the rest. So, much of the meat would appear on our tables as chopped meat, or sometimes only as a meat sauce, when we were lucky enough to have any meat at all.

Another important detail was made up of the chef's assistants, who peeled and prepared the vegetables, cooked the grain, and did whatever else was required to prepare the food for consumption. A small group of elderly men who were too weak to do much else were on the fly-swatting detail. With homemade swatters they stayed in the kitchen and dining room, stalking the pests and dispatching them. The men's toilets were right next to the kitchen so this was an important health-preserving task. Women were assigned to the grain-cleaning squad, and to the group that kept the floor clean.

To fill the long hours when not working for the common good of the camp, almost everyone had private projects, such as altering living space in the dormitories, fashioning sandals, making junk jewelry, and other private make-work. Of course weapons of any sort were forbidden, but few indeed were the prisoners who did not make knives from old automobile leaf springs. After they were made, they were carefully hidden from the guards. String belts were not merely ornamental, but were necessary to decency. Three years without a chance to purchase clothing caused us to look more than a little frayed around the edges, and most of us had lost so much weight that the rags which served us as trousers had to be tied to our waists.

Every now and then, as though to show who was in charge, the commandant would have his soldiers stage a surprise visit to the dormitories. They would tramp through, strip an occasional bed to see what might be hidden there, leaf through our books, and be off.

The afternoons were usually free of camp chores. After the midday heat had abated some of the men would organize baseball games. At first, the teams were made up of men from the same walks of life, such as miners, missionaries, professional men, etc., but the missionaries had the best pitchers and the strongest batters and won so routinely that we were broken up, and the captains then chose players without regard to their vocations. After that we had much closer games.

CHAPTER XX

At roll call one morning, there was much consternation among the guards when they discovered that one of the internees did not respond to his name. We knew at once that he must have "gone over the fence" during the night. Some of us had expected this, because Richie Green held a commission in the U.S. Army reserves, and we knew that the reservists had been biding their time until General MacArthur's inminent return made reactivation of their units possible. Also, one of the women had been frantically knitting socks for Richie against the time when he might have to do some campaigning in the jungles beyond the camp fences. So we were not as startled by his absence as were the Japanese.

After several rechecks, the commandant was reluctantly forced to conclude that Green had indeed left. He told us that this was a "very bad business" and that "the foolish man" would surely be recaptured and executed.* He further announced that to prevent anyone else from following this "stupid" example, he had decided that in the future, one of the male internees would have to stand guard with the Japanese soldier each night, and if the morning roll call showed that anyone had escaped during the night, the internee who had been on guard duty at that time would be summarily executed.

This proved to be an effective preventive, for no one wanted to be responsible for the execution of a fellow prisoner.

Not many of the soldiers assigned to guard duty had any knowledge of English so the nights were long as the silent pair of guards tramped slowly around the barracks in uneasy partnership, sitting down occasionally to rest and perhaps to smoke one of the cigarettes which came out of relief packages sent by the Red Cross sent. (During our 33 months of internment, we received only three such packages. We learned later that the Red Cross sent one package each month for each internee, regardless of age or sex. Each package contained several cans of C rations, a can of butter, and several packs of cigarettes. In most cases the Japanese did not convert the undelivered packages to their own use—they simply stacked them in a warehouse and neglected to pass them out to the prisoners.)

---

*Green reached his old outfit and ended the war as a full Colonel.

132

It was my good fortune to be assigned to guard duty one night with a Japanese soldier who had an excellent command of English. I learned that he had been a student at St. Paul's University in Tokyo. He was eager to practice his English and we carried on a lively conversation in whispers throughout the hours of patrolling. When we rested, we sat at the base of the parade ground flagpole, far enough away from the barracks so that we could converse in normal tones.

My good luck continued the next night I was on duty, for I drew the same companion. I learned that this infantryman had been wounded in the original assault on the beaches of Luzon, and after a spell in the hospital he was assigned to the less arduous task of guarding prisoners.

"We at the guard house know that you are getting news from the outside," said my companion after a bit of small talk. "We know that you have heard reports of American victories in the Pacific. So, you think you are winning, but you must realize that this is only the first battle of a war which will continue for many years. We Japanese will finally win."

"Many years?" I repeated in dismay. "How long do you think the war will last?"

"Do you know your European history? When the Dutch won their independence from the Spanish, the war lasted 80 years. And there was the 'Hundred Years War' in England. Perhaps this war will last as long. I think so. Fighting, peace, quarrels, fighting again. Another long truce, then more battles. No matter how long it takes, in the end we will win."

"I find that hard to believe," I protested. "War is too costly and we have much greater wealth than Japan. Our resources will make the difference, and we shall win."

"Ah, not so," my friendly enemy contradicted; "you see, it is Japan's ambition—no, that is not the word—it is Japan's *destiny* to rule the world. Because it is our destiny, it is also our duty."

In spite of the blackness of the velvet night I could see the sincerity and intensity of his convictions in his eyes.

"First we will conquer all of Asia. There we will find rubber, oil, iron, food, and all the other resources we need. Then when we have organized the Greater East Asia Co-Prosperity Sphere to our advantage, we will be ready to fight you again. You Americans upset our original plans. You forced us into the war before we were ready. That is why you are winning this first battle."

"We forced you?" I echoed in disbelief. "It was the Japanese bombing of Pearl Harbor that started the war. We did not attack you!"

"No, no," explained the soldier in patient tones such as a teacher might employ in making a point clear to a dull pupil, "you don't understand. You were strangling our lines of trade, You, and the British, the Chinese and the Dutch—the ABCD powers. You were preparing to crush us. Who fired the first shot is not important. The blame belongs to those who provoke the attack. And America is at fault. History will be written that way!" Here he smiled wryly, "Because we will write the history books."

We had made the circuit of the building several times and no one seemed to be trying to escape, so we were now sitting at the base of the parade ground flagpole. The guard was grateful for the American cigarette from one of my rare Red Cross relief packages.

"Yes, you forced us to fight before we were ready and we were unprepared. But we are a patient people, we Japanese. We shall wait 20, 30, 40 years, and then the story will be different. We shall then have much more strength. We shall have many more men because all the armies of Greater East Asia will be under our command. And the next time we shall not be so gentle. We shall kill every man, woman and child who stands in our way!" By this time his patient tones had given way to a ferocity which frightened me.

He took a deep drag on the cigarette, and as though I were not there, he ruminated, "It may take 100 years, but it is our destiny to win. The world must not be ruled by cowards. You Americans are cowards. I know, I have fought you on the battlefield. Your men fight from behind rocks and trees. You laugh at our Banzai charges. But men who have the courage to make those charges will eventually win the war."

Once again we circled the barracks, and then returned to the flagpole where we did not have to keep our voices down.

"I tell you something you have not seen," said the soldier. "When our commanders decide to take a hill, and they know that it will require 100 men to hold it, they send out 1000. Never mind the artillery, the mines, or the machine guns. Maybe 900 men will die in the charge. They are proud to die for the Emperor. But 100 men will survive, and the hill will be ours. Are your soldiers so brave? No. What do you say and teach your children? 'He who fights and runs away will live to fight another day.' A proverb for cowards! Our children learn another proverb: 'Better the arrow pierce your chest than your back.' Maybe you and I will not live to see the end of the war, or even of this first battle, but in the end my country will conquer the world. It cannot be otherwise. Japan has never lost a war."

In the years which have passed since this conversation took place, I have often wondered if it was simply the emotional outburst of a patriotic Japanese soldier, or if it truly represents the inner convictions of the millions of veterans of what the guard described as merely the first battle in a new hundred years war.

Perhaps the soldier with whom I stood guard that night, and

whose words still live in my memory, has come to realize, if he still lives, that his ferocious cry for a continuation of hostilities until a military victory might be achieved by Japan was puerile, and quite unnecessary. I hope that by now he has seen that the same spirit which enabled 1000 of his companions in arms to charge through a killing curtain of bullets so that 100 might occupy their objective has, channeled into ways of peace, made it possible for his nation to rise from defeat—that what Japan's generals and admirals could not accomplish by force of arms, her manufacturers and businessmen have brought to pass without bloodshed.

CHAPTER XXI

In the third year of our internment, rumors which could not be ignored bolstered our hopes that the end of the war, for us, was fast approaching.

We had known for some time that the American forces had landed in Leyte, but that was far to the south of Luzon. From a high point in the Camp through which we could see the blue of the China Sea and a small stretch of the lowland province of Ilocos Sur, we thought from time to time that we saw flights of planes swooping low over the arterial highway which ran alongside Lingayen Gulf, but it was too far away for us to have any certainty about the identity of the planes.

The big event came on November 25, late in that third year. At 8 a.m on that memorable day a small squadron of planes passed directly over our camp. One of the fighters peeled off from the formation and dropped low enough that we could see clearly that it was one of ours. Women screamed in delight, children jumped up and down and men shook hands and slapped each other on the back as though they personally had engineered the return of American planes to the skies over Luzon. Some Japanese guards raised their rifles and fired futilely at the daring pilot.

The official camp news sheet, posted daily on the bulletin board, usually confined its news reports to such momentous facts as to whether the principal meal would consist of mouldy rice or gravelly corn meal mush, and whether the morning beverage would be the second, third, or fourth "submarine coffee." (It was only when the coffee grounds could no longer tint the water in which they were boiled that they were discarded.)

Yet on the next morning, in giving the weather report for the day, the editor had dared to write, "Well, bless our trichromatic bunting and stellar spangled apple dumplings if this isn't turning out to be another balmy day. Why, Sinbad's great Roc couldn't find a better day to perform one of his ovipositions."

The Japanese interpreter no doubt struggled long and hard over these polysyllabic words before recommending to the camp commandant that the whole paragraph be deleted. It was.

It was nevertheless obvious to us as we peered through the gap in the mountains to the west that the Americans were, indeed,

136

taking advantage of the sunny day to deposit their lethal eggs on the arterial highway leading from Manila to the beaches of Lingayen.

Our camp committee held an emergency meeting and decided, on the basis of well confirmed reports which had come in over the fence, that the invasion of Luzon by the Americans could not be far off, and that the rumors about the abandonment of the camp must be credited. Even the least military-minded of us could figure out that when General MacArthur's forces landed on the Lingayen beaches they would drive east to cut the Island in half, thus preventing the hordes of Japanese in the south from reinforcing the northern units.

It was equally obvious that the Japanese would not want several hundred Americans, as weak and helpless as we were, behind their lines. Nor would they want us to escape into the mountains to reinforce the guerrillas or to seek refuge in the city of Baguio.

The committee decided also that as soon as definite word was received from the guard house that we were to be moved, we would slaughter our pigs, goats, and poultry, which we had been saving against the day when our rations would cease altogether. The cooks were notified that they should be prepared to cook the meat and to pass it out to the inmates of the camp prior to our departure, and that all flour of whatever sort should be baked into breads and biscuits for similar disposition. Now it became a matter of waiting for the removal order.

Our third Christmas in camp was marked gastronomically by generous meals. Breakfast consisted of a double portion of boiled rice, a dessert spoonful of brown sugar, real coffee, and a banana. (Bananas were now selling for two pesos each, Tokyo-printed military money.) For lunch we had corn meal mush served with camotes and onions. At dinner we had hamburgers made of a mixture of beef, carabao and horse flesh, rice, gravy and a candied camote. The candying was ingeniously accomplished by the cooks saving the water in which the camotes had been boiled and rendering it to a syrupy consistency. This was then splashed over the tubers. We had all enjoyed better Christmas dinners, but we were nevertheless most grateful to our kitchen staff for the trouble they had taken to produce a special meal with so little raw material.

The day after Christmas the camp commandant officially informed the camp committee that we would leave Camp Holmes the next day. He said that each internee would be allowed half a cubic yard of freight, but that only personal belongings might be taken along. He expressly forbade us to take any bedding or mosquito netting, because these items, he declared, would be found in abundance at our destination, which he still refused to name.

We were told that there would be 35 trucks assigned to the task of moving us south. All day long on the 27th of December we turned our private hoards of cassava, corn and rice flour into breads, and we packed, discarded, and repacked our meager supplies of clothing, secreting in the folds precious diaries, our Bibles, even our homemade knives, and such mementos as we knew would not take up much room.

At four a.m. on December 28, we had breakfast. As we passed the counter where the servers dispensed our mush and submarine coffee, the head of each family was given a chunk of boiled or roasted meat and a small amount of bread, which we were told would have to be our food allowance until such time as we arrived at our destination.

We then gathered our precious belongings and waited on the parade ground for the arrival of the trucks. Shortly after seven a.m. 19 vehicles arrived. The guards supervised the loading of these with freight and passengers and then told those of us who had not been able to board that we would have to await the arrival of more trucks, "maybe later today, maybe tomorrow." My wife, two little girls, and I were among those left behind. The rest of the day was anticlimactic. We wandered through the deserted barracks, saddened by the mass of material left because of freight limitations. The cook scraped together a meal of sorts late in the afternoon, and we wondered how our fellow internees were faring on their trip south.

The next morning we were roused again at an early hour, given a slim breakfast and told to wait for the arrival of the trucks. They appeared at about seven a.m. and we heaved our luggage aboard.

One of our number, a missionary, called us all to attention. He suggested that in view of the unknown dangers ahead, we ought to start our journey with a prayer. We solemnly commended ourselves into God's hands and then scrambled aboard whichever truck carried our own luggage, and the journey started.

As we followed a circuitous route through Baguio, obviously so that as few of the citizenry as possible would see us, we were told by the armed guards riding with us not to attempt any communication with people we might see. But no one could prevent us from responding to the Churchillian "V" for victory signal made by almost all those we saw on the roadside. We, too, raised our first two fingers in the sign, and the smiles on the faces of the people reassured us that we still had their loyalty and affection. We sped down the Kennon Road, a marvel of mountain highway engineering, but we could tell that our driver was not as expert as we would have preferred.

When we reached Binalonan in the Province of Pangasinan, we were ordered out of the trucks and told that we could rest and eat our lunch there. Kind Filipinos who tried to give us bananas and papayas were driven away by the guards. In peace time it would have taken two hours to accomplish this much of the journey, but we had been on the road for seven hours. There were two reasons for the slow trip—the road conditions and the movement of hundreds of Japanese soldiers to the north. The roads were pockmarked with bomb craters and we often had to leave what had been the hardtop road and make our way slowly through adjacent fields. Whenever Japanese military trucks came from the south, we had to pull over to the side and allow them to pass. Even foot soldiers had the right of way.

When we were forced to stop, our driver, a very weary little private who had been on continuous driving duty for the past three days ducked into the shade under the truck, stretched out, and fell fast asleep. When the road was clear, the sergeant in charge of our truck hauled him out of his resting place and we were off once again. That the poor chap was in no condition to drive was obvious. The truck would veer wildly to one side of the road, teeter on the edge of the ditch, and we would as with one voice scream. This awakened the chauffeur who would set the truck on its proper course until in a few minutes the near-wreck would occur again. One such time a fellow rider scolded me, saying, "Why didn't you shout with the rest of us to keep the driver awake?" I replied that I was too busy praying.

Apart from the lunch stop at Binalonan, there were no further rest stops allowed. If one had to answer a call of nature, he or she simply worked his way to the back of the truck and did the best he could over the tailgate. Three years of close confinement with scarcely any privacy in Camp Holmes had taken from us all traces of modesty, and no one seemed to suffer embarrassment when we relieved ourselves in this fashion.

In peacetime one could not have driven this road without scattering poultry, pigs, dogs and squeaking calesas drawn by skittish ponies. And there would have been numerous children playing on the road. But the Japanese occupation, during which the Army had lived off the land for three years, had left the countryside bereft of most animals, and the children were too undernourished to have energy for play. So we rolled along as fast as the northbound military traffic and the potholes would permit, passing through Capas, Tarlac and Bamban. But we skirted around San Fernando, perhaps because it was too large a town and the memories held by the populace there of the Death March from Bataan to Camp O'

Donnell were still vivid enough to raise the possibility of demonstrations.

By this time it was dark and our driver was even less capable of holding his vehicle on the road than he had been 12 hours before. Finally, when we actually did run off the road into a field, the sergeant made the driver climb down from his cab and stand against the side of the truck. Then with both hands he administered the most vicious face slapping I have ever seen. We felt sorry for the poor little driver, but we were not sure whether he was being disciplined or simply awakened. Whatever the motive, it worked, and from there on to the end of the journey we had no more careening from side to side.

Finally, at about one a.m., we rumbled through the streets of Manila into the courtyard of old Bilibid Prison. This complex had been condemned by the Philippine Government as being unfit for human habitation before the war. Its condition had not improved, but the Japanese considered it ideal for their prisoners.

When we were told to descend from the truck, we needed no urging. Some of our companions who had made the trip the day before were on hand to greet us. They told us that we would live in a large room with a concrete floor serving as our bed.

When we had retrieved our luggage we gathered again and uttered heartfelt thanks to God for our safe arrival at our new "home." One of the gold miners who had been on our truck stood to one side and then contemptuously declared, "I haven't said any of your goddam prayers, and I arrived safely, too." One of the missionaries replied imperturbably, "Yes, you rode in on our coattails."

The miraculous ride was over. That it was indeed a miracle we found later when we were told that the transit had taken place during the only three days when it was possible to move without being bombed. During those few days after Christmas there was a shortage of aviation fuel in the Philippines so no bombing raids were conducted. Of course the Japanese who had ordered the abandonment of Camp Holmes at that time did not know that, nor did the Americans know that there were 500 American civilians on the highway at that time.

Bilibid had recently been used by the Japanese as a stockade for captured American soldiers whom they crowded into the grim old prison while selecting those, who, in their opinion, could stand the trip to the Japanese or Manchurian coal fields. Those left behind were the physically unfit, the seriously ill, and the amputees.

Nevertheless they were the lucky ones because the majority of those who started on the voyage north perished. According to the best available records approximately 1600 of these POW's were crowded into a Japanese freighter, the *Oruku Maru*, which had been pressed into service as a transport, and only 250 of them reached their destination. By this time in the war American submarines were freely roaming Japanese waters and were torpedoing every Japanese craft they sighted. The *Oruku Maru* was one of those sunk. Prisoners who had not died of thirst, suffocation or disease, or of drowning when their ship was sunk, and who managed to escape the sharks and reach the beaches, were quickly recaptured by Japanese soldiers and sent on to their forced-labor assignments.

We had arrived from Baguio in the predawn darkness and there were no lights in the building to which we were directed. Groping blindly, someone found a heap of mattresses, and shouted the news of his discovery. Within a few minutes every mattress had been claimed. I didn't get one, so we bedded down on the concrete floor, all four of us huddling under a torn mosquito net I had packed into the blanket roll we had been allowed to throw onto our truck.

The light of day revealed a most unpleasant fact, especially for those who had been "lucky" enough to get bedding. The mattresses, as well as being filthy with the stains of excrement of men who had used them while slowly dying of fever and dysentery, were alive with vermin. Our camp committeemen took one look at them and had them all hauled into the courtyard where they made a spectacular bonfire. Our captors didn't like this at all. They said that we were most ungrateful. Even without lying on infested mattresses, the nights were a torment because of bugs which in the daylight hours inhabited the cracks in the walls and floors, but at night moved over onto us. That, and the unyielding concrete of the floor, made the nights most uncomfortable. It was not until the Americans recaptured Manila and brought in truckloads of canvas cots that we were able to sleep in comfort.

Daylight showed us something else, too. The white-washed plaster walls of the two large rooms to which we had been assigned were stained and cracked and shabby. But they were covered with graffiti. As we read these scribblings we could sense the desperation the writers had felt. They usually began with a man's name, his home address, his serial number and the outfit to which he belonged, then recited a record of his service from the time of his induction into the armed forces up to the time of his imprisonment in Bilibid. One biography ended with the pathetic query, "And now where? We hear we are moving out. God help us."

When Manila was recaptured by General MacArthur's soldiers, great care was taken to preserve whatever information could be gleaned from these scrawled graffiti. Only thus was the fate of scores of men learned.

In our new concentration camp, each family was permitted appro-

141

ximately 40 square feet of floor space. Manila was scorching hot, yet our water was rationed. Food was served only twice a day, and consisted for the most part of a coarse corn meal mush. The only outdoor space was a small concrete courtyard, and a well occupied cemetery in which there were many too shallow graves occupied by the bodies of American soldiers who had not made the trip to Japan nor to the military section of the prison. The days were long, and there was nothing to do. But we knew that time was running out for the Japanese. They knew it, too, and the knowledge made them increasingly surly.

We surely would have shared their bad humor had we known that the Japanese Supreme Command in Tokyo had told the internment camp commandants that they were to execute all internees rather than surrender them to any liberating forces. The date for our execution had been set for Monday, February 5, 1945.

General MacArthur was informed of this plan by a Japanese employed by U.S. Army Intelligence, and it was because of this that he sent two detachments of men, troopers from the First Cavalry Division, and infantrymen from the Thirty-second Ohio Division, by different routes, with orders to get to Manila as quickly as possible. They were to avoid contact with Japanese troops if possible, and dash into Manila to liberate the two internment camps, the one at Santo Tomas University, and the other at Bilibid Prison, in which we were guests.

Because the Japanese soldier lived under strict discipline and individual initiative was frowned upon, our camp commandant did not think he had the authority to advance the date of execution. So we lived.

It was with dramatic suddenness that liberation came. At sunset on February 3, some of us were on the roof of Beri-Beri Palace, as we called our prison building, looking at the usual spectacle in the western sky. (No place in the world has sunsets as magnificent as . those on Manila Bay.)

Suddenly we saw an even more beautiful sight—a column of vehicles coming into the city from the north. There were open trucks, weapons carriers, jeeps, and tanks, about a dozen or 15 in all, and they were American! When they arrived at the northern limits of the city, they were greeted by gunfire, and they responded with much more than they had received. From our vantage point we could see that they were racing apparently aimlessly around the several city blocks.

Actually, they were doing a splendid job of confusing the Japanese, who, at ground level, could not estimate the strength of the armored column which had hit the city. In panic and confusion the Japanese fell farther and farther back until they had withdrawn completely from the north end of Manila.

We did not see the end of the battle, for guards quickly appeared and chased us off the rooftop. Our commandant had been anticipating this day, and he gathered his garrison and waited for the Americans to come to Bilibid. They released our sister camp, Santo Tomas, first, and then they liberated the military section of our prison. We could hear the shouts of glee from the other side of the wall, and as the street fighting continued through the night, we wondered when would come our turn.

It was not until dawn on February 4, that the liberators learned that 500 civilians occupied the back part of the prison. Their officers and our commandant negotiated through an interpreter for safe conduct to their own lines for the Japanese garrison, in return for their pledge not to harm the civilian internees.

Then the great gate was swung open and in poured the most beautiful human beings we had ever seen. They were dirty, sweaty, tired and terribly grim from the street fighting but every one of those soldiers looked like an angel to us.

One great burly chap picked up our Penny, another our Jane, and the first cried out to the second, "Hey, Chuck, now I know why we've been fighting through those stinking jungles in New Guinea and all the way up here." Kissing the bewildered little girl, he said, "This is why. I've got a kid just about her age at home."

One of our internees was watching a group of boys as they sat and shared chocolate bars with emaciated prisoners. "That blond boy looks a lot like my brother," she said, turning to me. "He looks *just* like my brother. My God! He *is* my brother."

It was a wild morning. Someone broke out a homesewn American flag. We all tried to sing the National Anthem. But the tears and the gulps and sobs of joy made us give up. I've never heard a crowd sing *The Star Spangled Banner* since that day that I haven't thought of those wretched skeletons, of whom I was one, alternately crying and laughing and shouting greetings and "I told you so's" to one another.

But the day of liberation was a day of tragedy for some. The Japanese lobbed shells into Santo Tomas and killed several internees. The Americans parked their trucks behind our walls, and Japanese artillery sent phosphorus shells into their midst, causing several more casualties.

By the evening of February 5, the day on which our execution was supposed to have taken place, our end of the city was aflame. The Americans gave us just a few minutes to climb onto trucks and we were whisked through the burning streets to the abandoned *Ang Tibay* shoe factory.

It was there that we had our first meal "under new management," and what a meal it was—real bread, real butter, cereal with sugar, meat for sandwiches and coffee, buckets of real coffee, or hot chocolate, if we preferred.

When the fire had burned itself out, not having touched our prison home, we were returned to Bilibid. But it was a sad homecoming. Thinking we had left the prison to go to a relocation center before returning to the States and that we had abandoned all that we had left behind during our hasty evacuation, the Filipinos in the neighborhood, who had themselves been burned out of their homes, had swarmed into the prison and had helped themselves to our blankets, our clothing, and everything that was not nailed down. We could scarcely blame them, but we were disappointed that having kept certain of our possessions for the past three years we should now at the very end have lost them all.

Even before the city of Manila was secured, General MacArthur made an inspection tour of Old Bilibid to see for himself the wretched condition in which we had lived. As he toured the camp, many internees trailed along. The General seemed particularly interested in the cemetery behind our building. I was close enough to him to hear him say to one of his aides as he bent over to decipher the name and date on one of the crude wooden crosses used as a grave marker, "Ah, Sergeant so and so—a good soldier, that man. He served with me on Corregidor. If only we could have reached Manila in time."

A few days after the General's inspection trip, Mrs. MacArthur came in to see and talk to our womenfolk. She brought many dresses which were eagerly seized by women who had been living in little better than rags for years.

Then the army quartermaster opened a storeroom in the prison, and we were soon sporting new outfits from heavy boots to barracks caps. Everyone was happy. Even the children's wardrobes were attended to, although most of them continued to look like the refugee ragamuffins they were.

Soon after our return to the States, I chanced to see a copy of the Smith College Alumnae magazine. It contained an article by a graduate of that institution who had been in camp with us. A photograph of the General on that inspection tour illustrated the article. I was interested in trying to identify the many internees who surrounded his small party in Bilibid. I had sorted them all out but one, and it was only after careful scrutiny that I was able to identify this last one as being myself. I was so emaciated and looked so cadaverous that I truly could not at first recognize myself. During internment I had lost 70 pounds, down to 105 pounds. It was a good thing that we spent several months in the Philippines under American patronage after our release, for had we gone home at once it would have been a distressful experience for our families and friends.

144

We had thought that our ordeal was over when the troops moved in. Actually, the battle for Manila merely began on that day, and for many days thereafter we sat in the middle of what proved to be the greatest artillery bombardment in the Pacific war. Night after night an officer would come in, and calling us to attention, he would tell us that we would hear much heavy shelling, but that he hoped it would all be going in one direction. "If any of you think you won't be able to sleep, the O.D. at the desk in the front hall will give you sleeping pills."

Dangers of a different sort now beset us. I was taking a shower one day and I heard a thud, then the sound of a shot. I looked behind me and saw that a bullet which had arrived before the sound of its firing had splintered an upright on which the shower head was fastened. I could see at a glance that the bullet had missed my head by no more than a few inches. I grabbed my towel, threw it around my middle, and dashed across the compound to the desk of the Officer of the Day.

I told him what had happened, and together, from the portico of the building in which his office was located, we could see that a supposedly empty building overlooked the wall of the camp and that it was the most likely spot from which the sniper had fired at me.

The officer called on the telephone and gave a quick resume of the story to the soldier on the other end of the phone. Within a few minutes a light, high-winged plane, the military version of a Piper Cub, I think, came buzzing over the building and dropped a fifty-pound bomb squarely on the building. Thus ended the career of one Japanese sniper. When we stand at God's Judgement Seat, if some Japanese comes forward and says, "Father of all Men, that priest was responsible for making my wife a widow," I shall reply, "Yes, but you started it! "

So far as I know, that enemy soldier is the only human being for whose death I am directly responsible. As the years have passed, and as my fright and anger have subsided, I would like to think that at the time my feelings were a mixture of regret that one of God's children had perished and relief that a threat to American lives had been eliminated. Deep down, however, I know that my initial reaction was one of unchristian satisfaction.

As soon as the streets were fairly quiet, Bishop Wilner and a few of us priests received permission to cross the city to the Cathedral. We wanted to retrieve such records as had not been destroyed in the bombardment and fire. We knew, too, that there had been left there in the vault urns containing the ashes of parishioners. These we wanted so that we could turn them over to kinfolk in the States.

It was a nightmarish trip. The Cathedral had been used as a stronghold by the Japanese. Corpses were strewn all over the floor, and mangy dogs were feasting on them. It was impossible to cross what would have been the nave of the Church without stepping on dead Japanese soldiers.

Burial squads were piling up bodies at various points in the city and trucks lumbered through the streets collecting them and stacking them like so much firewood. Manila, which had been so beautiful with its marble and granite public buildings, was a pile of rubble.

But we were alive. And soon we would go home. Or so we thought. We had forgotten the ways of the Washington bureaucrats.

Some bright lad in the State Department required us all to sign vouchers and I.O.U.'s promising to pay the U.S. Government the price of a first-class passage across the Pacific, even though it was evident that our voyage home would be aboard a military transport. However, he reckoned without the fiery General MacArthur, who, when he heard this, demanded that all those slips of paper be destroyed and said that if the Government insisted on the repayment of passage money, it be charged to his personal account. He knew too, that transport was in short supply due to the imminent invasion of Okinawa and the necessity of ferrying hundreds of thousands of fighting men to that strongly held Japanese redoubt. Nevertheless, because of his conviction that the presence of American civilians in the Philippines throughout the war, even though imprisoned, had helped keep the Filipino morale high and thus made his task of reconquest easier, the General cut through miles of red tape and secured transports for our camp inmates.

We envied those who sailed before us out of Manila for San Francisco, but we knew our turn would come. So for six weeks we continued to live in our all but deserted camp.

During this time an Army doctor examined us in an effort to rescue, for immediate evacuation by plane, those whose physical condition was so poor that they needed proper medical attention in hospitals in America.

Florence was found to be suffering from two nutritional diseases, beri-beri and pellagra. The treatment prescribed was a properly balanced diet and a supplemental dosing with vitamins. My problem was emaciation. So the enforced delay in our repatriation proved to be a blessing in that we were both able to regain some of our health while waiting and eating.

This regimen went on for six weeks on Manila. Eventually the authorities decided to send those who had not found passage on the first transports to Leyte, in the hope that transportation from there to the States would be arranged sooner. So we all were flown down to Tacloban on the island of Leyte.

But the campaign for the conquest of Okinawa had begun and all transports were being used to ferry combat soldiers. Repatriating American civilians enjoyed low priority.

In Leyte our women and children were housed in a convalescent hospital while the men found lodging in a rotation and replacement camp.

For another six weeks we lolled around in Leyte. We rested. We ate. We bathed on the sundrenched beach. We ate some more. We visited in the hospital and the camps. We were entertained by the U.S.O. And we kept on eating. Florence recovered quickly, and I put some flesh on my skeleton because of the gluttony we were committing daily.

It was during this waiting period that letters which had piled up in Geneva, and fresh ones written after word of our release had reached the States, began pouring in. There was so much family news to catch up on. For some it was sad to find out that death had visited the homefolk, or that younger members of the family had been killed or wounded in battle. For others there was joyous news of marriages and births.

It was on Easter Day in 1945 that I had the thrill of having first hand news of my family. A GI found me in my tent and identified himself as Louis Kusin, a friend of my sister in Louisiana. He told me that my brother was an officer in the U.S. Navy, and had been invalided home from Guadalcanal, but was well on the road to recovery and that I should not head for New York upon reaching the States because my parents, who until word of our liberation had reached the States had heard nothing from or of us since our capture in 1942, had moved to Louisiana in 1944 to be near my sister and her family. He then loaded us into a weapons carrier which he had commandeered and drove us to his company's camp where we joined his fellow soldiers in a sumptuous Easter feast.

When one of the servers on the chow line greeted us in a friendly and voluble fashion, Florence responded at once by saying, "Oh, you are a coal cracker from Pennsylvania!" The startled GI agreed that her reading of his accent had correctly identified him. He lived only a few miles from Pottsville, where Florence had several aunts and cousins. We took his name and upon our visit to that area later on we made it a point to see his parents, and to assure them that Patsy, the fourth of their four sons in the military service, was alive and well.

It was not until early May that we boarded the *M/S Gaspara*, a Dutch ship under contract to our armed forces. The officers were not happy to see our contingent come aboard. It meant that they had to give up their quarters to the women and children. The men were tucked into bunks erected in the tanks which in days of peace had carried copra and oil. They were not comfortable accommodations, but as long as the vessel was headed west, we didn't care.

The ship also carried many GI's returning to the States—men who had been wounded or who were due for home leave. Within a few days all of the children had found their own particular soldiers who most willingly assumed the task of caring for them during the daylight hours.

Janie, our younger daughter, was much freckled, and one day her GI asked, "Janie, where did you get all those freckles?" She looked bewildered for a moment and then responded, "From the Red Cross." All her clothes and candy and other goodies had come from that agency, so Jane, then four years old, naturally ascribed everything she had to the single benefactor she knew.

We reached San Francisco the day after V-E Day, looking well fed, tanned and healthy. But we weren't really. I wanted to return to the Far East as a Naval Chaplain, but I was told that I would not be able to pass the physical, and that even if I did squeak past the examining doctors, I would probably be assigned to a stateside post.

The Church asked me to spend some time travelling around the country reporting on the destruction of the fabric of the Mission in the Philippines, and raising money for the Reconstruction and Advance Fund. In the year following I preached or lectured just over 300 times and sent thousands of dollars back to the Philippine Mission.

When finally the Church released me from this task, I reported for my physical preparatory to returning to the Islands. The doctors rejected me as being too fatigued and nervous.

All the while I was out on the road, I told people that I would be returning to the Philippines as soon as possible.

However, the doctors in the Mission Board's office had other ideas. They said that my chest X-rays showed that I had been suffering from tuberculosis while in camp. The lesions had calcified and all tests for T.B. were now negative, but the doctors said they could not approve of my return to the missionary field for some time to come.

CHAPTER XXII

The years passed. We lived in Long Island where I served as Director of Christian Education for the Diocese of Long Island and as Rector of St. Thomas' in Bellerose, and where Christopher and Peter, our two sons, were born in 1946 and 1949, respectively. From there I went to St. Augustine by the Sea in Santa Monica, California, as Rector. In 1961 I was called to St. Paul's in Kansas City, Missouri. It was while I was serving this Parish, one of the largest west of the Mississippi, that in recognition of the work which I had done in the Philippines the General Theological Seminary awarded me the degree of Doctor of Sacred Theology.

Wherever we made our home, from time to time we had the joy of entertaining Igorot Churchmen as they visited in the States. Some came as official delegates of the Philippine Church to Episcopal Conventions, some came as exchange students. But we rejoiced that all seemed to think a visit to America would be incomplete without dropping in on *Apo Padi*.

It was a strange contrast to the days when an Igorot could not leave the Mountain Province without a special pass. The people who in the early part of the century had been listening to distant drums were now marching to the same beat that sounds in our ears.

"Apo Jesu Kristo" was no longer an imported Lord of a small cult. The Igorots were giving their best sons and daughters to His ministry, ordained and unordained. Pushed along by the events of World War II considerably faster than anyone might have predicted earlier in the century, the Church in the Philippines had reached maturity. The Igorots, with more volunteers for the ministry than were needed to man their own churches, were now going forth as missionaries themselves to their racial kinsmen in North Borneo and to the Filipinos in Hawaii.

Early in 1965, something which Florence and I had dared dream might some time happen became a reality. We found that we could make a return trip to the Islands.

The timing of our trip was determined by a series of unrelated circumstances, but it worked out most fortunately. We reached Manila on the thirty-third anniversary of my ordination. By a happy coincidence, the annual convocation of the Church was in progress. This drew to Manila members from all over the Archipelago. At

149

no other time in the year could we possibly have seen so many of our old friends, white and brown, without extensive travelling, which our schedule did not permit.

The Bishop, the Right Reverend Lyman Ogilby, the last American to serve in that post, graciously invited me to preach at an ordination service. Three lads who had not been born when I had last been in the Islands were advanced to the priesthood. To see two Filipino Bishops, Benito Cabanban and my former interpreter, Edward Longid, both of whom had been in my first seminary class in 1932, participating in the service, and to see a score of Igorot priests, some of whom I had also instructed, was thrilling.

But it is not only in the Church that the Igorot has stepped out of his primitive villages and taken his place in the bustling world of today. Doctors, educators, administrators, legislators, and public officials, including the elected governor of the Mountain Province, were all on the roster of old school pupils upon whom we called as we revisited our old home.

The Governor of the Mountain Province, Alfredo Lamen, whom I remembered as a little Igorot boy in our mission school, told me that shortly after his election he had participated in a political rally in Vigan, a town where the majority of residents were lowland Filipinos. Before appearing on the platform, he said, he had stepped into a small room, divested himself of his western clothing, and donned a loincloth.

Then he had stepped out on the platform and said to the people, "You have come to hear the governor speak. Perhaps you are wondering where he is, what he looks like, and what he will say. In years past you Ilocano people of the lowlands said that the Igorot was like a monkey, with a long tail. But an Igorot has now prevailed in a free election, and has been chosen to the highest office in the Province. I am he. I am your governor," and twirling the ends of his g-string, he added, smiling broadly, "and these are the only tails any Igorot has." At first, he said, the crowd sat in shocked silence. Then it broke into laughter and cheers for their Igorot Governor.

Within a year of our return visit the American Bishop of the Philippines resigned his office and Bishop Benito Cabanban, the senior Suffragan Bishop, took his place. Soon after, the Diocese was divided and Bishop Edward Longid, also a Suffragan, became the first Bishop of the new Diocese of the Northern Philippines, which included the Mountain Province.

The dreams of dozens of American missionaries, many now dead, were realized. The Philippine Episcopal Church was now functioning with an indigenous Episcopate and Priesthood. *Apo Padi* was no longer needed.

PICTORIAL SECTION

(Note: Except for the last two pages—164-165—of pictures in this book, all other pictures are from the "postcard" collection of EDUARDO MASFERRE for which use permission was obtained with the help of William Henry Scott. Grateful acknowledgment is hereby given.)

The famous rice terraces

Road between Sagada and Bontoc

View of Sagada (1952)

View of Bontoc (1952)

St. Theodore's Hospital in Sagada where Dr. Clapp often assisted the resident missionary doctor.

St. Mary's High School, Sagada

St. Mary's High School, Sagada

St. Mary's Church, Sagada

Inside St. Mary's Church, Sagada

Preparing the soil before planting

Harrowing the field in preparation for planting rice

Young lad's task—pasturing the family carabao

The planting season is a season for work, dancing and singing.

Victory dance after a raid on an enemy village

Bontoc war dance

In full regalia for a head-hunting trip.

A watch party high over the narrow trails could easily command all entries to Sagada.

Age, rather than knowledge, was venerated among the illiterate Igorots.

(Gang-awan of Sagada)

Kiwang of Sagada

Ornaments identify her as a Kalinga lady.

Igorot

W o m e n

Apo Padi and his horse Mazla (August 1932)

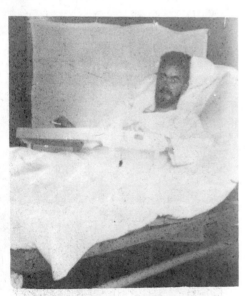

Apo Padi as appendectomy patient at St. Luke's Hospital, Manila (August 1933)

Visit to Upi and Zamboanga Mindanao (1939)

St. Paul's School in Samoki, Mt. Province (1940)
(Fr. Nobes at the back with faculty member)

e Nobes family (Florence,
nie, Clifford, and Penny)—
me at last! (May 1945)

SOME RELATED NEW DAY BOOKS

Ancheta, Celedonio A. THE WAINWRIGHT PAPERS (4 vols.)
Bundok, Pedro. DEMOCRACY AMONG THE MOUNTAINEERS
Cortez, Rosario M. PANGASINAN: 1592-1800
Cullamar, Evelyn T. BABAYLANISM IN NEGROS: 1896-1907
Dumia, Mariano A. THE IFUGAO WORLD
Fry, Howard T. A HISTORY OF THE MOUNTAIN PROVINCE
Gleeck, Lewis E., Jr. THE AMERICAN GOVERNORS-GENERAL
    AND HIGH COMMISSIONERS IN THE PHILIPPINES
    DISSOLVING THE COLONIAL BOND
Gloria, Heidi K. THE BAGOBOS
Gowing, Peter G. MANDATE IN MOROLAND
    MUSLIM FILIPINOS—HERITAGE AND HORIZON
    UNDERSTANDING ISLAM AND MUSLIM IN THE
    PHILIPPINES
Jenista, Frank L. THE WHITE APOS
Kerkvliet, Benedict J. THE HUK REBELLION
Kikuchi, Yasushi. MINDORO HIGHLANDERS: THE LIFE OF THE
    SWIDDEN AGRICULTURISTS
May, Glenn A. A PAST RECOVERED: ESSAYS ON PHILIPPINE
    HISTORY AND HISTORIOGRAPHY
    SOCIAL ENGINEERING IN THE PHILIPPINES
Ochosa, Orlino. THE TINIO BRIGADE
Pal, Agaton & Robert Polson. RURAL PEOPLE'S RESPONSE TO
    CHANGE
Salamanca, Bonifacio S. THE FILIPINO REACTION TO
    AMERICAN RULE
Santiago, Luciano. THE HIDDEN LIGHT: THE FIRST FILIPINO
    PRIESTS
Scott, William Henry. CRACKS IN THE PARCHMENT CURTAIN
    DISCOVERY OF THE IGOROTS
    ILOCANO RESPONSE TO AMERICAN AGGRESSION
    1900-1901
    PREHISPANIC SOURCE MATERIALS FOR THE STUDY OF
    PHILIPPINE HISTORY
    A SAGADA READER
Shalom, Stephen R. THE UNITED STATES AND THE PHILIPPINES
Warren, James. AT THE EDGE OF SOUTHEAST ASIAN HISTORY
    THE SULU ZONE: 1768-1898
Wolters, Willem. POLITICS, PATRONAGE AND CLASS CONFLICT
    IN CENTRAL LUZON

Build up your own Filipiniana collection by checking with your favorite bookstore in Metro Manila for the above titles, or contact NEW DAY PUBLISHERS (P.O. Box 167, 1100 Quezon City, or Tel. 99-80-46). Subscriptions to the UPPER ROOM (English, Cebuano, Ilocano, and Tagalog editions available) are also accepted.

In the United States, the official distributor for New Day books is THE CELLAR BOOK SHOP, 18090 Wyoming St., Detroit, MI 48221.

FROM THE AUTHOR

After more than half a century, memories fade, so I cannot properly thank the scores of people who contributed to the fullness of the life I try to recall in these pages.

However, I can never forget the part that Bishop Edward Longid played. He was one of my first students, but he taught me far more than I taught him. He instructed me in the language of the Igorots and in the mysteries of their culture, but far more importantly, I learned from him how to minister to them so that they, too, could know the joy of discipleship in the service of God.

The preparation of a manuscript for submission to a publisher is a long and tedious process. I was spared much of this by a sympathetic and efficient friend, Mrs. Christian (Hortense) Nicholsen. "Horty" had the difficult job of deciphering my scrawl and turning in into a neat typescript. I will be forever grateful for her help and her friendship.

Finally, my nephew, Ralph Talbot Troy did a heroic job for me. Ralph advised me on what to include, what to exclude, and what to reword. He retyped reams of pages and patiently put up with my many changes of mind in the course of writing this history; then, when the manuscript was completed to our satisfaction, he set about finding a publisher. His determination to see his uncle's story in print was rewarded with success, so to him belongs a major share of the credit for *Apo Padi* becoming a book.

Clifford E. Nobes